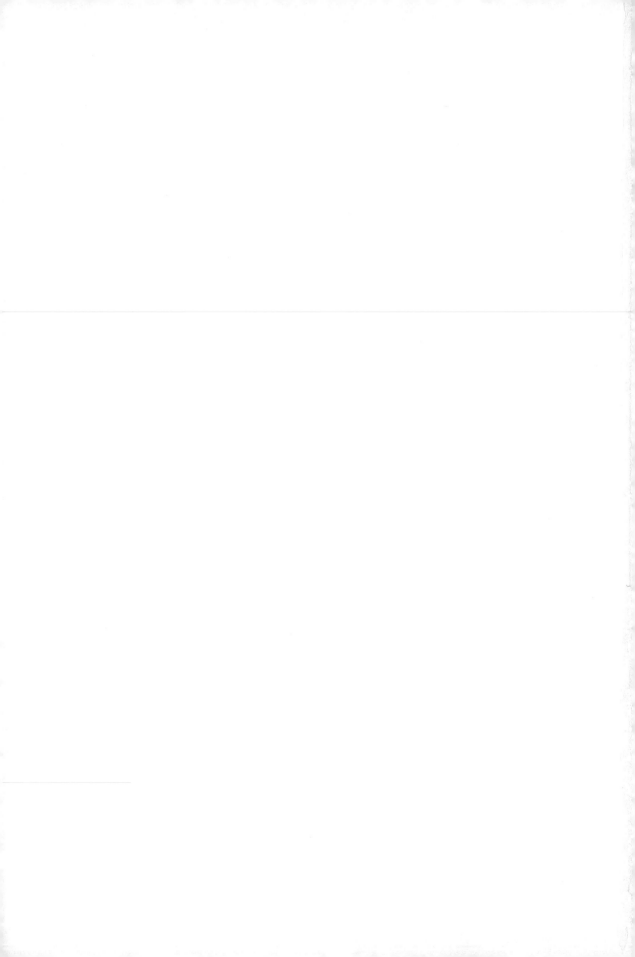

THE CATFISH CONNECTION

BIOLOGY AND RESOURCE MANAGEMENT IN THE TROPICS SERIES

Michael J. Balick, Anthony B. Anderson, and Kent H. Redford, Editors

Biology and Resource Management in the Tropics Series
Edited by Michael J. Balick, Anthony B. Anderson, and Kent H. Redford

Alternatives to Deforestation: Steps Toward Sustainable Use of the Amazon Rain Forest, edited by Anthony B. Anderson

Useful Palms of the World: A Synoptic Bibliography, compiled and edited by Michael J. Balick and Hans T. Beck

The Subsidy from Nature: Palm Forests, Peasantry, and Development on an Amazon Frontier, by Anthony B. Anderson, Peter H. May, and Michael J. Balick

Contested Frontiers in Amazonia, by Marianne Schmink and Charles H. Wood

Conservation of Neotropical Forests: Working from Traditional Resource Use, edited by Kent H. Redford and Christine Padoch

The African Leopard: Ecology and Behavior of a Solitary Felid, by Theodore N. Bailey

Footprints of the Forest: Ka'apor Ethnobotany—the Historical Ecology of Plant Utilization by an Amazonian People, by William Balée

Medicinal Resources of the Tropical Forest: Biodiversity and Its Importance to Human Health, edited by Michael J. Balick, Elaine Elisabetsky, and Sarah A. Laird

THE CATFISH CONNECTION

Ecology, Migration, and Conservation

of

Amazon Predators

RONALDO BARTHEM & MICHAEL GOULDING

COLUMBIA UNIVERSITY PRESS   NEW YORK

Columbia University Press
Publishers Since 1893
New York   Chichester, West Sussex
Copyright © 1997 Columbia University Press
All rights reserved

Library of Congress Cataloging-in-Publication Data
Barthem, Ronaldo.
    The catfish connection : ecology, migration, and conservation of
  Amazon predators / Ronaldo Barthem and Michael Goulding.
        p.   cm. — Biology and resource management in the tropics series)
    Includes bibliographical references and index.
    ISBN 0–231–10832–X (cloth)
    1. Pimelodidae—Amazon River Watershed.   2. Catfish fisheries—
  Amazon River Watershed.   I. Goulding, Michael.   II. Title.
  III. Series: Biology and resource management in the tropics series.
  QL638.P6B37   1997
  597'.49—dc21   96–47920

Casebound editions of Columbia University Press books are printed on
permanent and durable acid-free paper.
Printed in the United States of America
c 10 9 8 7 6 5 4 3 2 1

Contents

Figures

Tables

Preface

For conservation biology it is important to understand to what extent animals might need huge areas for their survival. The Amazon Basin is the largest rainforest and river system in the world. Until the present work there was no solid evidence for animal species either requiring or using a large part of the Amazon Basin to meet their ecological needs. Any such animals would almost certainly be migratory, the most likely suspects being fishes and birds, given the long-distance migratory patterns of many other species in these groups elsewhere in the world. (Insects should not be dismissed, but we know too little about their migratory patterns to understand how far they might travel within the Amazon Basin.) We know that birds from North and Central America and southern South America make seasonal migrations to the Amazon Basin, but how resident and nonresident birds migrate within the basin is still largely a mystery. Are distinct parts of the region tied together ecologically by avian life cycles? As for mammals, there no records of any species making long migrations in the Amazon Basin. The giant river turtle (*Podocnemis expansa*) might travel long distances to nest on beaches, but its movements are not as obvious as those of fishes and birds and would be extremely difficult to trace without tagging experiments.

For about fifteen years we have suspected that some of the large catfishes in the Amazon—especially the species called piramutaba and dourada in Brazil—might use most of the large rivers of the lowland areas and the estuary during their lives. This area embraces at least 2,500,000 km^2 and a 4,000-km axis measured along the Amazon River. It also includes most of the large tributaries of the western half of the Amazon, a region that includes Brazil, Colombia, Peru, and Bolivia. In this work we present strong evidence supporting this thesis, based on an extensive database and field observations of Amazon catfish migrations. We believe that the species involved ecologically connect a large part of the Amazon Basin, especially through their reproductive cycles and food-web relationships. When entire life cycles are considered, piramutaba and dourada appear to make the longest migrations of any freshwater fish species in the world.

Dourada and piramutaba are among the five most important food fishes in the Amazon Basin. The long-distance migratory behavior of these large catfishes is probably the main reason for their abundance. During their evolution these species have dispersed widely in Amazonian rivers and the estuary. Their feeding habits allow them to assume predatory roles in various habitats, and until recently their migratory behavior enabled them to diminish predation on themselves. But now the large catfishes are facing a major predator: Since the 1970s uncontrolled commercial fisheries have been heavily exploiting them. Populations living in the estuary, from which upstream fish are eventually recruited, have been heavily exploited by industrial operations; this is especially true for the piramutaba. Piramutaba fisheries are now threatened with commercial extinction unless immediate steps are taken to manage them.

The purpose of this book is to outline the ecological nature of the estuary and river-channel catfishes in the Amazon, to examine their exploitation by commercial fisheries, and to suggest what steps need to be taken to protect some of the most fantastic animals on Earth. The "catfish connection" defines a new ecological size for the Amazon. The responsibility needed to protect the catfish resource is as large as the ecosystem that these animals embrace.

Acknowledgments

For financial help we are especially indebted to the following institutions and people: the Museu Paraense Emilio Goeldi (MPEG), the Rainforest Alliance, the Conselho Nacional de Desenvolvimento Científico e Tecnológico (CNPq), the W. Alton Jones Foundation, the Tinker Foundation, the Superintendência de Desenvolvimento da Amazônia (SUDAM), the Financiadora de Projetos e Pesquisas (FINEP), the Instituto Nacional de Pesca y Aquicultura (INPA), the Instituto Nacional de Pesquisas da Amazônia (the National Institute of Amazonian Research, or INPA), the World Wildlife Fund (WWF-US), the Sociedade Civil Mamirauá (SCM), Judy Sulzberger, Joel Edelstein, and the Norcross Foundation.

For their professional help, we thank the following people: Daniel R. Katz (Rainforest Alliance), Márcio Ayres (Museu Goeldi and the Wildlife Conservation Society), Guilherme de La Penha (former director of the Goeldi Museum), Pete Myers (W. Alton Jones Foundation), Thomas Lovejoy (Smithsonian Institution), José Seixas Lourenço (Secretário de Coordenação dos Assuntos da Amazônia Legal), Renate Rennie (Tinker Foundation),

Rosemary Lowe-McConnell, Adélia Engrácia de Oliveira (Museu Paraense Emilio Goeldi), Heraldo Britski (Museu de Zoologia, University of São Paulo), Naércio Menezes (Museu de Zoologia, University of São Paulo), José Lima (Museu de Zoologia, University of São Paulo), John Lundberg (Arizona State University), Miguel Petrere Jr. (University of São Paulo), Richard Vari (Smithsonian Institution), Stanley Weitzman (Smithsonian Institution), Sven Kullander (Swedish Museum of Natural History), Leo Nico (National Biological Survey), Raimundo Aragão Serrão (Museu Paraense Emilio Goeldi), Karin Kreider (Rainforest Alliance), Jeff Richey (University of Washington), Helene Weitzner (Rainforest Alliance), Efrem Ferreira (Instituto Nacional de Pesquisas da Amazônia), Antonio Carlos Gonçalves da Silva, Fernando Gonçalves da Silva, Raimundo Sotero da Silva (Instituto Nacional de Pesquisas da Amazônia), Lázaro Campos (FRIUBA), Paulo Taketomi (EDIFRIGO), Sigueru A. Esashika (Mamirauá Civil Society), Maurício Valderrama (Instituto Nacional de Pesca y Acuicultura), and Estácio Gomes (Colônia dos Pescadores, Zê Santana).

For criticisms of the manuscript we thank: Rosemary Lowe-McConnell, Donald Stewart, Richard Vari, and Diego Muñoz-Sosa. We also thank Peter Bayley for extensive discussions on Amazon fish ecology over the years.

The fishermen who helped us are too numerous to list here, but we would like especially to acknowledge the help of the late Aderson da Silva, former employee of the National Institute of Amazonian Research, who spent three years collecting data for us before his untimely death at a young age.

THE CATFISH CONNECTION

1

Introduction

When most people think of predators in the Amazon, piranhas and jaguars probably come to mind first. But a far more profound and far-reaching predatory network has evolved in the large river channels and estuary. Most of these predators are large catfish, some of them extremely important in the commercial fisheries of the inland waters and the estuary. In this work we present strong evidence for a "catfish connection" that ecologically links the lowland rivers of the Amazon and the estuary. At least two species of Amazon catfish can probably claim the longest migrations known for any species in any river system in the world. This has profound implications for fisheries management and conservation programs.

Large catfish are important food fishes in the Amazon, but almost nothing has been done to manage the fisheries based on them. In fact, so little is known about their life cycles that any management plan would have been mostly guesswork. Some biologists also feel that it might be too expensive and difficult to maintain the high yields of these species taken by commercial fisheries in the 1970s and early 1980s (Bayley 1981; Bayley and Petrere Jr. 1989).

Although total catches cannot be maintained at the levels recorded in the late 1970s, we believe that the two most important catfish species—dourada and piramutaba—can and should be managed to prevent their commercial extinction. We will explain how this might be done in the concluding chapter.

This study is an investigation of predation, including fisheries, and what needs to be known about it to better exploit and manage predators on which people depend for food. The channels of the Amazon River and its main tributaries have about a dozen large predators: a shark, sawfish, several species of stingrays, two species of dolphins, and catfish. Beyond any doubt the most abundant species are catfish, and only they are commercially important. (Some of the stingrays might be more common than indicated by fisheries, but they are exploited relatively little because of poor markets for them.) This book will focus mainly on catfish because of their abundance and importance in the commercial fisheries and also because we now know more about them than the other fish species. A brief overview, however, of most of the diversity of the large predators found in the Amazon River can be found in chapter 2.

PERIOD OF STUDY

This study uses data collected between 1976 and 1995. Examining the life cycles of the large catfishes represented a challenge born initially from curiosity, and we were not at all sure that we could get enough information to fulfill our purpose. For the most part, we collected data on them while focusing on estuary and floodplain ecology.

The main problem we faced was that fishermen did not understand catfish migrations beyond individual fishing areas and no one had seen or reliably reported the whereabouts of spawning grounds or larval fish. It took us approximately a decade of intensive (though not exclusive) fieldwork to locate the fry and juveniles of some of the species and to get sufficient measurements of specimens captured from migratory schools. We still have not located the young of about half of the large catfish species. Some species seem to be so rare that is it amazing that these animals find each other to reproduce.

COLOMBIAN AND PERUVIAN STUDIES

Our studies were restricted mostly to Brazil, though we were aware in the late 1970s that dourada and piramutaba migrate upstream as far as Colombia, Peru, and Bolivia. Colombian and Peruvian biologists began to collect seasonal data on large catfishes in their respective countries in the 1990s. Of the long-distance migratory species, only the dourada has been studied in any detail in Peru or Colombia. The data collected by Muñoz Sosa (1993) in Colombia and Salinas (1994) in the Colombian and Peruvian border area strongly suggested that dourada spawn in the upper Amazon Basin. By the process of elimination, based on our investigations in the estuary and most of the Brazilian Amazon, along with the Colombian and Peruvian data, it became evident to us that spawning takes place mostly if not exclusively in the western region.

STUDYING MIGRATION

For most species that move long distances, migration and reproduction are intimately linked. Small-scale tagging experiments that have been attempted in the Amazon have not been successful, and at present none are being tried (for attempts, see Godoy 1979). Neither of us has tried to tag Amazon fishes to determine their migratory patterns. We believe the value of such experiments in an area as large and unknown as the Amazon is doubtful and would be too expensive in the absence of general models that can offer initial hypotheses. The models we present should serve as a basis for future tagging experiments for at least two of the catfish species that migrate from the estuary to inland waters.

As an alternative to tagging experiments, we have compared fish length and species composition in various rivers of the Amazon Basin during different seasons of the year. Nearly sixty thousand specimens were measured in markets, on commercial fishing boats, or during scientific expeditions. We supplemented these data with measurements of specimens taken in experimental fishing. The stomach contents of over ten thousand specimens were also examined. Most of the specimens studied were captured by commercial fishermen. We also surveyed approximately twenty-five rivers to determine the distribution of predators and prey and also the whereabouts of fry and juvenile fish (figure 1.1). Our fish collections are deposited in the Museu de Zoologia of the University of São Paulo and the Museu Paraense Emilio Goeldi in Belém.

THE AMAZON REGION

Following the rainforest limits, the Amazon region embraces eight countries, 6,112,000 km^2 and accounts for about one-third of South America (figure 1.2). The Rio Tocantins is not a tributary of the Amazon River, but it is linked to it biogeographically and ecologically and is extremely important to the estuary.

FIGURE 1.1
Main Sites Where We Have Made Fish Collections in the Amazon Basin

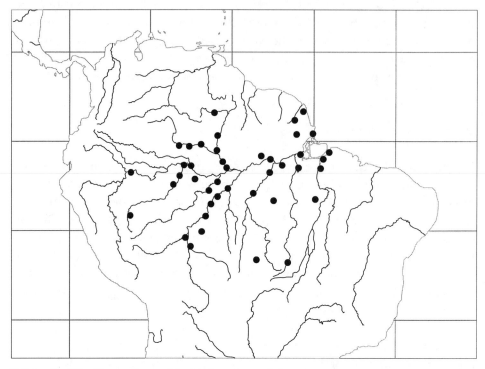

With the Rio Tocantins added, the size of the Amazon region increases to 6,869,000 km² (COPRAPHI 1984). Most of the Amazon region is found in Brazil (68%), though none of the Andean headwater regions are. Nearly all of the drainage from the Brazilian and Guiana Shield areas is in Brazilian territory. The entire estuarine area is in Brazilian territory. As we argue in the conclusion, international cooperation will be essential for managing large catfishes in the Amazon, as nursery habitats appear to be confined to Brazil for some of the species and spawning areas may embrace four countries.

THE AMAZON RIVER

The Amazon is the largest river system in the world. Its headwaters are born at nearly five thousand meters on the icy slopes of the Andes in Peru and flow at least 5,890 km before reaching the Atlantic (Barbosa 1962; Salati et al. 1983). Its name changes seven times in the three countries through which it flows. Born as the Rio Apurimac, it flows 800 km until its confluence with the Rio Mantaro, at which point it is called the Rio Ene. After the confluence of the Rio Ene and

Rio Perene, some 150 km downstream, the Rio Tombo is formed, and it flows another 150 km until meeting the Rio Urubamba and transforming into the Rio Ucayali. The Rio Ucayali meanders 1,500 km through lowland Peru until it meets the Rio Marañon, when it becomes the Rio Amazonas (in Colombia as well) until it enters Brazilian territory at the mouth of the Rio Javari. In Brazil the Amazon River is called Rio Solimões above its confluence with the Rio Negro; downriver it is called the Rio Amazonas. The Brazilian Rio Solimões-Amazonas is nearly 3,000 km in length, from the Colombian/Peruvian border to the Atlantic. In Brazilian territory the Amazon River receives waters from over a thousand tributaries, several of which are more than 1,500 km in length, such as the Rio Madeira, Rio Purus, Rio Juruá, Rio Tapajós, and Rio Xingu.

River levels in the Amazon are controlled by rainfall over a broad region of the basin, not by snow melt in the Andes. Average annual precipitation is over 2,100 mm, and annual rainfall reaches 8,000 mm in some of the eastern Andean areas (Day and Davies 1986). The hydrological cycle in the Amazon Basin is heavily influenced by the vast rainforest, which recycles approximately one-

FIGURE 1.2
The Amazon River Basin

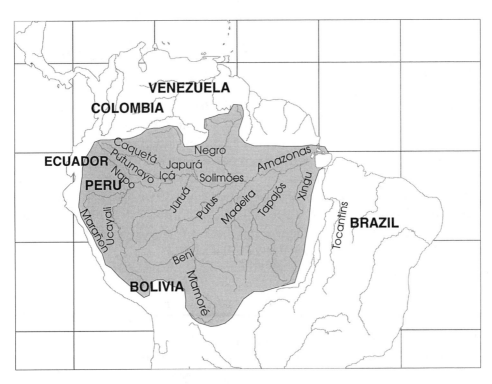

half the precipitation that falls on it. The rainforest in effect stabilizes the hydrological cycle and decreases runoff (Salati and Vose 1984).

Rainfall in the Amazon Basin varies greatly both seasonally and geographically. In terms of latitude the Amazon River flows between about 4 degrees south in Peru and the equator, which passes almost exactly through the mouth area. Amazonian tributaries stretch from 15 degrees south to nearly 4 degrees north latitude. Because of different rainfall patterns, each year the southern tributaries begin to flood several months earlier than do their northern counterparts. The upper Rio Madeira, for example, begins to rise in late October or November, whereas the upper Rio Negro only begins to rise rapidly in March or April. The northern tributaries usually have a small flood in October or November, but this passes rapidly, and river levels do not rise more than two meters. The different seasonal contributions from the southern and northern tributaries cause the Amazon River to stay in flood longer than would otherwise be the case (Meade et al. 1991). In most years the Amazon is rising very rapidly by January or February, and the floodplains become heavily inundated. Although the southern tributaries begin to fall in March or April, the Amazon River remains in flood until August because of swollen northern tributaries. The lower reaches (200–300 km) of both the southern and northern tributaries have the same level as the main river because of its damming effect. This phenomenon is very important because it causes large areas of floodplain to remain inundated for five to seven months each year, thus increasing total aquatic productivity.

Annual river-level fluctuation varies considerably in the Amazon because of geomorphological differences in channel shape and floodplain topography. In the Andean foothills, rivers fluctuate less than in most of the Central Amazon. At Iquitos, Peru, the Rio Amazonas fluctuates on average about seven meters (figure 1.3). Near Manaus, the Rio Solimões-Amazonas fluctuates about ten meters. Farther downstream, the Rio Amazonas at Óbidos only fluctuates on average about five meters. River-level fluctuation in the estuary is controlled by the daily tides and averages about four meters.

The Amazon River discharges about one-fifth (6,700 km^3) of all river water that enters the oceans each year (COPRAPHI 1984). This is equivalent to five times the discharge of the Zaire, the second-largest river in the world (Milliman and Meade 1983). High-water discharge can exceed low-water discharge by more than 250 percent (Meade et al. 1991).

THE GEOLOGICAL AND BIOLOGICAL BACKDROP

The principal geological regions that have affected and still influence the chemistry of Amazon rivers are the Andes, the Brazilian and Guiana Shields,

FIGURE 1.3
Water-Level Fluctuation at Various Points in the Amazon

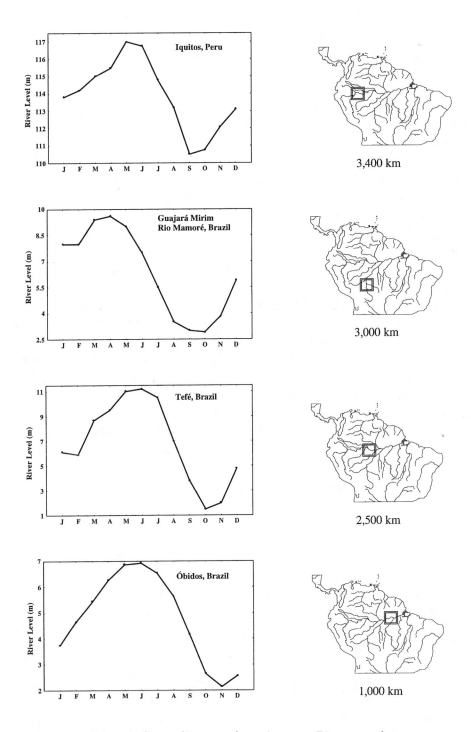

Maps indicate distances from Amazon River mouth.

and the main Amazon sedimentary basin. The exact details of the formation of the Amazon Basin are still poorly known. The most important relatively recent geological event affecting the Amazon River was the rapid rise of the Andes in the middle and late Miocene, perhaps fifteen million years ago. Most geologists agree that the Amazon changed its direction of flow after this event. Hoorn, Guerrero, and Sarmiento (1995) suggest that the Amazon once fed the paleo-Orinoco river system, which drained toward the Caribbean. As early as the late Miocene, however, the Orinoco connection was closed and an Atlantic connection was opened. The Andes blocked drainage to the west, and the Amazon River cut through the low-lying area near Santarém, where the Brazilian and Guiana Shields met. If fossils of the large catfishes that now migrate to and from the Amazon River estuary were to be found in western Peru or Ecuador, that would strongly suggest that these species migrated to Pacific coast estuaries before the rise of the Andes (none of the extant Amazon River catfishes are found west of the Andes). It would also suggest that the Amazon River once flowed to the Pacific as well.

Owing to copious precipitation in the Andes, along with the high elevation of the mountain chain, there is very heavy erosion. This erosion becomes expressed in the rivers as muddy water. The entire Amazon River is rendered turbid from the Andes to the Atlantic. It delivers approximately 0.8 to 0.9 billion tons of sediments to the Atlantic each year, most of which comes from the Andes, four thousand or more kilometers to the west. The superficial geomorphology of floodplains along the Amazon, and of other muddy rivers such as the Rio Madeira, Rio Purus, and Rio Juruá, is formed by the Andean sediments that have been deposited during the annual floods. The Andes have complex rocks as a result of volcanism and other orogenic processes, thus the eroded sediments supply either in solid or dissolved form a relatively rich nutrient base to the rivers that carry them away. In overall nutrient content, the Amazon is slightly richer than the world average for large rivers (Gibbs 1967).

Brazilians refer to the sediment-rich rivers of the Amazon as whitewater rivers, in order to contrast them with the two other main types: clearwater and blackwater rivers (figure 1.4). To avoid confusion, we will refer to whitewater rivers as muddy rivers. Clearwater rivers have low sediment loads, are poor in nutrients, and originate mostly on the highly eroded Brazilian and Guiana Shields. Blackwater rivers flow from drainage basins whose soils consist mostly of quartz sands and where there is very little erosion. Organic compounds from forests are incompletely decomposed in sandy soils, and the leftover residue stains the waters into which they are carried. Most of the non-Andean tributaries in the western half of the Amazon Basin are blackwater rivers, the Rio Negro being the largest. They are extremely poor in nutrients.

FIGURE 1.4
The Meeting of the Rio Amazonas (Muddy Water) and Rio Tapajós (Relatively Clear Water).

This image illustrates the great contrast in water types found in the Amazon Basin.

The sedimentary basin through which the Amazon River flows covers about 2 million km² and was reshaped various times during the Cenozoic. The sediments filling the depression are mostly from the ancient Brazilian and Guiana Shields and, to the west, from the Andes. The sedimentary basin has sunk under the weight of its own materials. The elevation at Manaus is only 40 m. Near Manaus parts of the Rio Negro mouth-bay are nearly 100 m deep, thus 60 m below sea level some 1,800 km upstream. About 3,000 km upstream, near Tabatinga, Brazil, and Leticia, Colombia, the elevation is still only 65 m. At Iquitos, Peru, 3,400 km upstream, the elevation is 110 m.

Three main components of the Amazon system are directly important to river predators: river channels, floodplains, and the estuary. The Amazon River channel varies in average depth between about 15 and 40 m (figure 1.5). The presence of islands and heavy sedimentation on the floodplains greatly reduces channel width, to an average of about 2 to 3 km. The river is usually split into several channels because of the presence of islands. High natural levees border the main river and are only inundated at the peak of the floods; however, large floodplain areas in back remain connected to the main river by channels that cut through the levees. Because of high turbidity and a strong if not swift current, phytoplankton production is low in muddy river channels; however, large amounts of organic matter, including parts of floating meadows, are washed into the channels from the floodplains (Junk 1970). Richey, Mertes, and Victoria (1989) estimate that about one-third of the water annually discharged by the mainstem is derived from water that has passed through the floodplain.

Midstream velocity of the Amazon River during the flood stage reaches a maximum of about 2 m/second, or 7.2 km/hour. River water moving at about 173 km/day takes approximately twenty days to travel from the eastern foothills of the Andes to the Atlantic. Near the levees and beaches the current speed is reduced to 0.1–0.4 m/second. The lower reaches of tributaries of the Central Amazon are held back by the main river for several months each year, thus their current speed is also reduced. In the case of the Rio Negro, for example, current speed averages only about 0.8–1.4 m/second, or 2.9–5.0 km/hour.

The low elevation through which most of the Amazon River flows has led to the development of large floodplains. The Amazon River does not meander greatly for most of its length, so it has relatively (but not absolutely) less floodplain than some of its tributaries, such as the Rio Purus. Large numbers of

FIGURE 1.5
Large Ship in the Amazon River Channel

islands, however, greatly increase the shoreline coefficient, that is, the proportion of shore habitat relative to river length. Most of the primary production that sustains fish communities takes place on floodplains. Flooded forests, floating meadows, and algae have all been cited as important sources of carbon for the foodchains on which Amazon fish communities depend (Goulding 1980; Bayley 1989; Araujo-Lima et al. 1986; Forsberg et al. 1993). Flooded forests and floating meadows cover at least one-half of the entire Amazon floodplain, though deforestation is now changing this ratio.

The Amazon estuary is formed by the Rio Amazonas to the north and Rio Tocantins to the south. Amazon River waters reach the southern part of the estuary through the Canal de Breves, which empties into the Rio Pará, a tributary of the Rio Tocantins (Barthem and Schwassmann 1994). The Rio Tocantins, whose lower reaches are muddied by Amazon River water, then empties into the Baía do Marajó. The northern and southern parts of the estuary are separated by the huge island of Marajó. Sioli (1966) defined the Amazon estuary at its Atlantic side as lying between Cabo Norte and Ponta do Tijuca, a distance of 380 km.

The mouth of the Amazon River does not form a delta. The Southern

FIGURE 1.6
Salinity Conditions in the Amazon Estuary During the Low- (right) and High-Water (left) Periods of the Amazon River

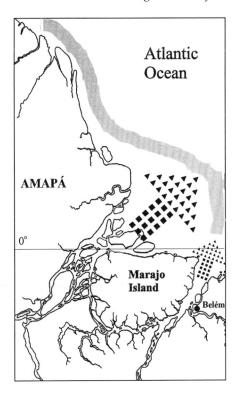
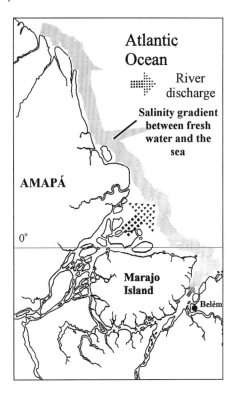

Equatorial Current displaces river discharge in a north-northwest direction, thus preventing the large-scale deposition of sediments. An internal delta, however, is formed by the large number of islands present, such as Marajó, Caviana, Mexiana, and Gurupá. The huge amount of freshwater discharged by the Amazon River greatly decreases salinity along the northeast coast of South America as far as Guyana (figure 1.6) (Ryther, Menzel, and Cordin 1967; Eisma and Marel 1971).

Tides extend as far up the Amazon River as Santarém, or nearly 1,000 km upstream. The reverse tidal current reaches the mouth of the Furo de Breves, 325 km upstream. Because of the enormous discharges of the Amazon River and the Rio Tocantins, the estuary is largely freshwater; this is clearly indicated by the present of floodplain rainforest on the inundated islands of the estuary. Mangroves, which only grow in the presence of brackish water, are found exclusively on the eastern edge of the estuary. Slightly saline water can be detected between 150 and 200 km upstream on the southern side of the estuary (Egler and Schwassmann 1962; Barthem and Schwassmann 1994). On the northern side, where the main river discharges, freshwater dominates 185 to 230 km out to sea (Diegues 1972; Curtin and Legeckis 1986). There is a broad mixing zone north and east of Marajó where algae production is very high. River water supplies the nutrients, either in dissolved form or through organic matter, and oceanic water offers the clarity for the light penetration needed for intense production. It is this area of high primary production that serves as the nursery for some large catfishes and many other estuarine animals as well.

2

Large Fishes of Amazon River Channels

This chapter gives a natural history overview of the large fishes found in the river channels of Amazonian muddy rivers. An essential part of this overview is to present length-weight relationships and the maximum size known in order to establish size classes, estimated ages, and population structures. All lengths are expressed as fork lengths, which is the distance between the end of the snout and the fork in the caudal fin.

Dourada (*Brachyplatystoma flavicans*, Pimelodidae)

See figures 2.1 and 2.2.

Common names:	dourada (Brazil), zúngaro dorado (Peru), dorado and plateado (Colombia)
Identification:	only large species with platinum head and gold body; only large species with short barbels when adult
Maximum known size:	192 cm
Range:	widespread in Amazon Basin; similar if not same species in Orinoco basin; passes rapids (e.g., upper Rio Madeira) and found as far as headwater regions of many tributaries (e.g., Rio Madeira and Rio Negro)
Habitats:	channels of large rivers, including muddy, blackwater, and clearwater tributaries; occasionally enters floodplains at night to feed but returns to channels before daybreak

SOURCES: Eigenmann and Eigenmann 1890, 1971; Goulding 1979, 1980, 1981, 1988; Barletta 1995; Zuanon 1990

FIGURE 2.1
Dourada (Brachyplatystoma flavicans)

FIGURE 2.2
Length-Weight Relationship of Dourada (N=1507)

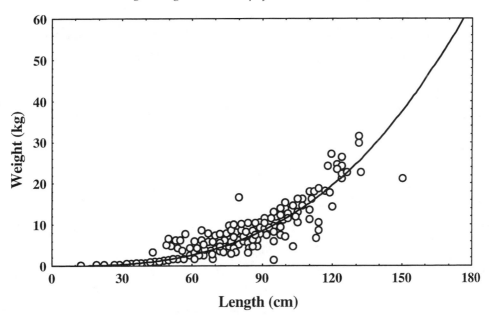

Piramutaba (*Brachyplatystoma vaillantii*, Pimelodidae)

See figures 2.3 and 2.4.

Common names:	piramutaba, pira-botão, and mulher-ingrata (Brazil); pirabutón (Colombia); manitoa (Peru)
Identification:	gray above, white below; large adipose fin clearly distinguishes the species from piraíba
Maximum known size:	105 cm
Range:	widespread in Amazon Basin, but usually not above first rapids except for the Rio Madeira; similar if not same species in Orinoco basin
Habitats:	channels of large rivers, including muddy, blackwater, and clearwater tributaries; in freshwater part of estuary; relatively rare in blackwater and clearwater rivers

SOURCES: Eigenmann and Eigenmann 1890, 1971; Mees 1974; Anonymous 1981; Barthem 1985, 1987, 1990a, 1990b; Dias-Neto, Damasceno, and Pontes 1985; Godoy 1979; Neto, Evangelista, and Freitas 1981

FIGURE 2.3
Piramutaba (Brachyplatystoma vaillantii)

FIGURE 2.4
Length-Weight Relationship of Piramutaba (N=321)

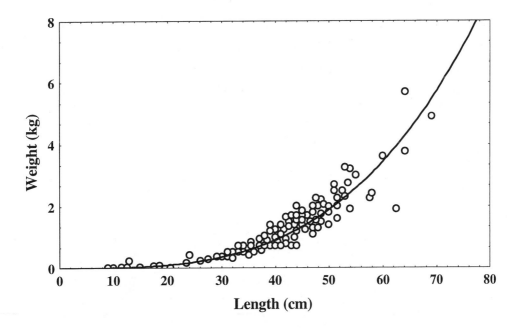

Piraíba (*Brachyplatystoma filamentosum*, Pimelodidae)

See figures 2.5 and 2.6.

Common Names:	piraíba, filhote (Brazil); zúngaro saltón (Peru); pirahiba, lechero, valentón (Colombia)
Identification:	probably more than one species, but most of the commercial catch taken in river channels appears to be of the same species; young fish called filhote in Brazil; no distinct color patterns (dorsal part of body is dark or gray, ventral area is whitish); when less than 60 cm in length, fish can be confused with piramutaba and even some members of the Ariidae in the estuary; a short adipose fin distinguishes this species from the piramutaba; from all other species, it is distinguished by the absence of a membrane connecting the two pairs of nares
Maximum known size:	280 cm
Range:	widespread in Amazon Basin; similar if not same species in Orinoco basin
Habitats:	channels of large rivers, including muddy, blackwater, and clearwater tributaries; in freshwater part of estuary; large populations of young fish found in floodplain waters as well as in river channels

SOURCES: Eigenmann and Eigenmann 1890, 1971; Goeldi 1897; Mees 1974; Goulding 1979, 1980, 1981, 1988; Barletta 1995; Zuanon 1990

FIGURE 2.5
Piraíba (Brachyplatystoma filamentosum)

FIGURE 2.6
Length-Weight Relationship of Piraíba (N=543)

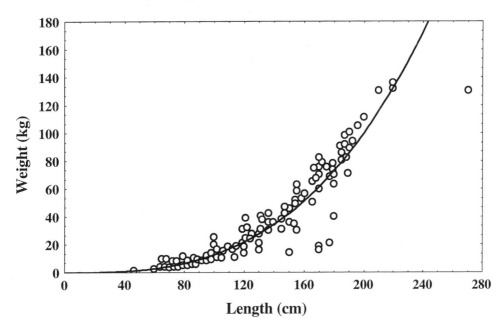

Zebra (*Brachyplatystoma juruense,* Pimelodidae)

See figures 2.7 and 2.8.

Common names:	zebra, flamengo (Brazil); siete babas (Colombia); zúngaro alianza (Peru)
Identification:	thick vertical to oblique stripes; easily distinguished from dourada zebra by large adipose fin and very short barbels
Maximum known size:	60 cm
Range:	widespread in Amazon Basin but usually relatively rare and not reported anywhere to be an important food fish
Habitats:	known in channels of muddy rivers only; not found thus far in estuary

SOURCES: Boulenger 1898; Goulding 1981

FIGURE 2.7
Zebra (Brachyplatystoma juruense)

FIGURE 2.8
Length-Weight Relationship of Zebra (N=33)

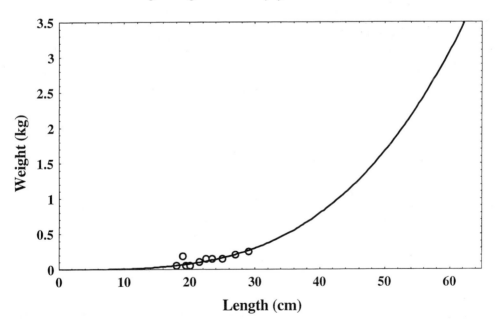

Surubim (*Pseudoplatystoma fasciatum,* Pimelodidae)

See figures 2.9 and 2.10.

Common names:	surubim, surubim-lenha (Brazil); pintado, rayado, pintadillo (Colombia); zúngaro doncella (Peru)
Identification:	vertical to slightly oblique black stripes; often has spots, which are thicker on the ventral side; great variation in stripe and spot patterns; Eigenmann and Eigenmann (1890) recognized at least fourteen varieties or subspecies based on color patterns; future revisions may divide surubim into several species; easily confused with caparari, even by fishermen in areas of the Amazon where the two species are found together, although the stripes and head of surubim are narrower
Maximum known size:	105 cm
Range:	very widespread in Amazon Basin but rare or absent from estuary; reaches headwaters of all river types, though different species might be involved
Habitats:	found in river channels, floodplains, and larger rainforest streams, in both running and still waters

SOURCES: Eigenmann and Eigenmann 1890, 1971; Goulding 1979, 1980, 1981; Reid 1983; Zuanon 1990

FIGURE 2.9
Surubim (Pseudoplatystoma fasciatum)

FIGURE 2.10
Length-Weight Relationship of Surubim (N=324)

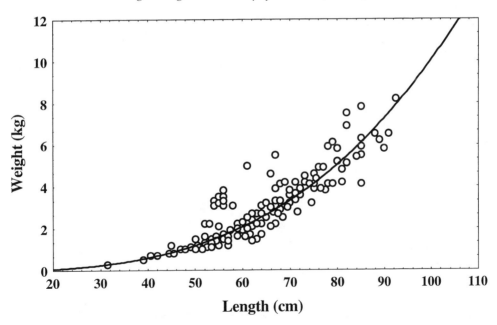

Caparari (*Pseudoplatystoma tigrinum,* Pimelodidae)

See figures 2.11 and 2.12.

Common names:	caparari (Brazil); bagre tigre (Colombia); tigre zungaro (Peru)
Identification:	vertical to slightly oblique stripes; easily confused with surubim, but see discussion above
Maximum known size:	125 cm
Range:	very widespread in Amazon Basin but rare or absent from estuary; appears to be much rarer than surubim in head-water areas
Habitats:	found in river channels, floodplains, and larger rainforest streams, in both running and still waters

sources: Eigenmann and Eigenmann 1890, 1971; Goulding 1979, 1980, 1981; Reid 1983; Zuanon 1990

FIGURE 2.11
Caparari (Pseudoplatystoma tigrinum)

FIGURE 2.12
Length-Weight Relationship of Caparari (N=350)

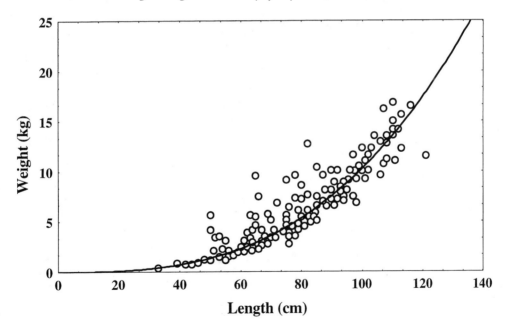

Babão (*Goslinia platynema*, Pimelodidae)

See figures 2.13 and 2.14.

Common names:	babão, xeréu, barba chata (Brazil); baboso, saliboro (Colombia)
Identification:	dark above, white to creamy ventrally; only species that is dark dorsally with no body spots and has very large and flattened barbels
Maximum known size:	100 cm
Range:	widespread in Amazon lowland areas, including estuary; not yet reported in any blackwater or clearwater tributaries
Habitats:	known only in muddy river channels and freshwater estuarine waters

SOURCES: Steindachner 1909; Myers 1941; Goulding 1979, 1981; Barthem 1985

FIGURE 2.13
Babão (Goslinia platynema)

FIGURE 2.14
Length-Weight Relationship of Babão (N=198)

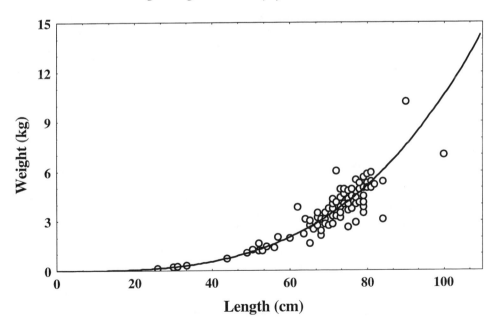

Peixe-Lenha (*Sorubimichthys planiceps*, Pimelodidae)

See figures 2.15 and 2.16.

Common Names:	Pirauaca, peixe-lenha (Brazil); cabo de hacha, peje leña (Colombia); acha cubo (Peru)
Identification:	strong vertical striping and only large species whose upper jaw far surpasses lower
Maximum known size:	150 cm
Range:	widespread in Amazon lowland areas; appears to be common only west of the Rio Tapajós; not yet reported in any blackwater or clearwater tributaries
Habitats:	known only in muddy river channels east of the Rio Tapajós

SOURCES: Eigenmann and Eigenmann 1890, 1971; Goulding 1979, 1981

FIGURE 2.15
Peixe-Lenha (Sorubimichthys planiceps)

FIGURE 2.16
Length-Weight Relationship of Peixe-Lenha (N=14)

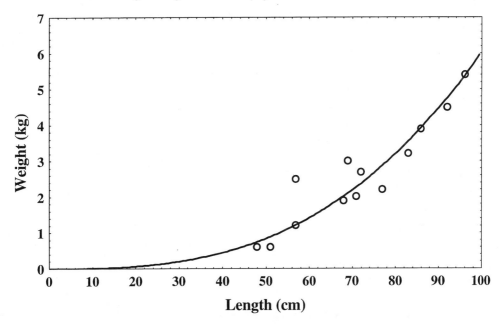

Pirarara (*Phractocephalus hemiliopterus*, Pimelodidae)

See figures 2.17 and 2.18.

Common names:	pirarara, bigorilo, guacamayo (Brazil), pirarara, guaca-mayo (Colombia); pez torre (Peru)
Identification:	only large catfish with bright orange tail and massive bony head
Maximum known size:	110 cm
Range:	widespread in Amazon and Orinoco basins, including blackwater and clearwater tributaries; reaches headwaters
Habitats:	river channels, floodplains, and western parts of estuary

SOURCES: Eigenmann and Eigenmann 1890, 1971; Goulding 1979, 1980, 1981

FIGURE 2.17
Pirarara (Phractocephalus hemiliopterus)

FIGURE 2.18
Length-Weight Relationship of Pirarara (N=47)

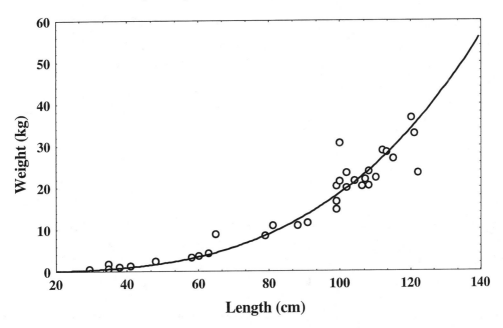

Jaú (*Paulicea lutkeni*, Pimelodidae)

See figures 2.19 and 2.20.

Common names:	jaú, pacamão (Brazil); peje negro, chontaduro, pacamu (Colombia); cunchi mama (Peru)
Identification:	only large catfish with greenish-gray body; short barbels
Maximum known size:	140 cm
Range:	widespread in South America if same species is involved; reported from northern Argentina to Venezuela, in all river types; often common in headwaters and near cataracts
Habitats:	river channels and floodplains; not reported in estuary

SOURCES: Ihering 1928; Goulding 1979, 1980, 1981

FIGURE 2.19
Jaú (Paulicea lutkeni)

FIGURE 2.20
Length-Weight Relationship of Jaú (N=37)

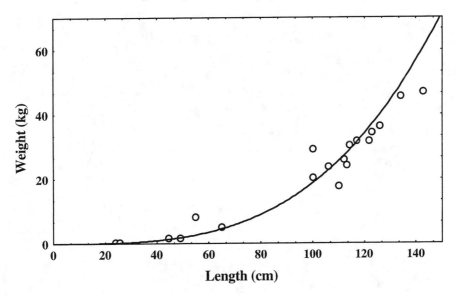

Coroatá (*Platynematichthys notatus*, Pimelodidae)

See figure 2.21.

Common names:	cara de gato, coroatá (Brazil); capaz (Colombia)
Identification:	only large catfish with numerous spots but no stripes; very large and flat barbels; great variation in color patterns and possibly more than one species involved
Maximum known size:	50 cm
Range:	widespread in Amazonian lowlands in all river types
Habitats:	river channels and floodplains; not reported in estuary

SOURCES: Eigenmann and Eigenmann 1890, 1971; Goulding 1979, 1980, 1981

FIGURE 2.21
Coroatá (Platynematichthys notatus)

Dourada Zebra (*Merodontodus tigrinus*, Pimelodidae)

See figure 2.22.

Common names:	dourada zebra (Brazil)
Identification:	only large catfish with highly oblique stripes; much shorter barbels than zebra, with which it can be confused
Maximum known size:	50 cm
Range:	known only from a few specimens from the upper Rio Madeira and Caquetá region of Colombia; species has also been photographed in the Santarém fish market by Efrem Ferreira of the National Institute of Amazonian Research
Habitats:	river channels of muddy rivers

SOURCES: Britski 1981; Goulding 1981; Castro 1984

FIGURE 2.22
Dourada Zebra (Merodontodus tigrinus)

Bullshark (*Carcharhinus leucas,* Carcharinidae)

See figure 2.23.

Common names:	tubarão, branco (Brazil); bullshark (English-speaking world)
Identification:	only shark in the inland waters of the Amazon
Maximum known size:	220 cm (in Amazon) but larger in ocean
Range:	widespread in Pacific, Atlantic, and Indian Oceans; known in freshwaters of several continents
Habitats:	in the Amazon known only in channels of muddy rivers

SOURCES: Myers 1952; Compagno 1984; Thorson 1972, 1973; Roberts 1972, 1973; Werder and Alhanati 1981; Barthem 1985

FIGURE 2.23
Bullshark (Carcharhinus leucas)

Sawfish (Pristis microdon, *Pristidae)*

See figure 2.24.

Common names: espadarte (Brazil); sawfish (English-speaking world)

Identification: Long sawlike rostrum

Maximum
known size: 140 cm (in Amazon) but larger in ocean

Range: widespread in Pacific, Atlantic, and Indian Oceans; known
        in freshwaters of several continents

Habitats: in the Amazon known only in channels of muddy rivers

SOURCES: Myers 1952; Thorson 1974; Barthem 1985

FIGURE 2.24
Sawfish (Pristis microdon)

3

Technology of Catfish Exploitation

FISHING CRAFT

Small-scale fisheries in the Amazon use diesel-powered boats ranging in size from less than a ton to at least seventy tons. Nearly all of them are constructed from wood (figure 3.1). Downriver of Santarém and in the estuary, sail rigging is common. Canoes are often used for subsistence fishing and near urban centers where catches can be delivered within a few hours.

Most of the ice boats used in the Lower Amazon or estuary have a capacity in excess of ten tons. Buyers follow fishermen seasonally to areas that are being heavily exploited. When captures are high, there is a symbiotic relationship between buyers and fishermen, as the fish must be iced quickly or it will spoil. During the main fishing season for piramutaba in the Baía de Marajó, for example, most fish are purchased by buyers with ice boats. Fishermen sell directly to buyers in return for money and goods. Buyers often supply food and fuel as incentives for fishermen to increase their catches. Buyers purchasing catches in situ pay less than half the price paid by urban markets.

FIGURE 3.1
Types of Boats Used in Small-Scale Fisheries of the Amazon Estuary

Ice boxes used on small boats are usually divided into various compartments, each of which can hold about one ton of fish. Fish are placed in layers separated by pieces of ice. Approximately one ton of ice is used for each ton of fish. At this ratio and considering the types of ice boxes used, fish can last a maximum of twenty days but are much better if sold within two weeks.

The highest prices paid for fish in the state of Pará are at the Ver-o-Peso market in Belém. Boats dock next to the market at high tide and remain during low tide as beached craft. Catches are rarely removed all at once but sold piecemeal to different fishmongers in order to attain the best price. In other towns and cities, however, catches are often sold to single buyers that distribute them to inland markets.

The fishing boats used in the interior of the Amazon rarely rely on sails and have a relatively shallower draft than do estuarine boats. Canoes are used extensively, either alone or as part of the fishing equipment of a boat. The largest boats found in inland waters belong to the Manaus fleet, and some of these have a capacity of seventy tons. Few exclusively exploit catfish but instead fish a variety of species, at least during the course of the year. Large catches of piramutaba and dourada are sold to export companies with refrigeration facilities. Only a small percentage of these catfish are consumed locally.

The industrial fleet operating in the Amazon estuary consists of approximately sixty steel boats 17–27 m in length, with individual storage capacity ranging 20 to 105 tons (figures 3.2 and 3.3). The average boat has a seven-man crew. All industrial boats operating in the estuary carry the Brazilian flag, although some of the fishing companies are supported in part by international investment, especially Japanese.

GILL-NET FISHERIES

Gill nets are the most important gear used by small-scale operations exploiting catfishes in both the estuary and inland waters. Gill-net types are the same in both areas, though they are used differently, as we discuss below. Because catfish live mostly in deeper waters, gill nets must be heavily weighted in order to sink to the bottom or to the desired depth. Depending on the species being fished, line strength and mesh size vary. Mesh sizes for piramutaba, dourada, and piraíba range between 12 and 20 cm. The larger sizes are used in river channels upstream of the estuary. The longest gill nets we have recorded in the estuary measure about 3,000 m. The maximum length used in river channels is about 800 m. Gill-net technology is now widespread, and most fishermen and their families know how to make them. There are also many outlets in urban centers that sell gill nets imported from the state of São Paulo.

The long gill nets used in estuarine fisheries are placed in the water from the bow of the boat. Because of rough waters and wind conditions, canoes are not used with gill nets in the estuary. Estuarine operations fish in accordance with the tides. At the beginning of low tide, fishermen put to sea in order to save energy by taking advantage of the strong oceanward currents. Return to port takes place during high tide. In the river-channel fisheries of the interior, gill nets are stretched from canoes rather than from the main boat.

Fishing in estuarine waters takes place in a much more uniform, or sealike, environment than inland rivers afford. Whereas in river channels piramutaba, dourada, and other catfishes can be spotted at or near the surface, rarely is this the case in the estuary. Instead, estuarine fishermen depend on past experience of where schools are at certain times of the year and on information gathered from coastal communities. They also look out for concentrations of seagulls. Fishermen know that amuré gobies (Gobioides spp.) are the principal prey of piramutaba, and many are killed but not eaten during predatory attacks. Dead or wounded prey rise to the surface and are then attacked by seagulls. In addition, the stench emanating from large numbers of dead gobies is perceptible from several kilometers when the wind is favorable. Finally, nearer to the site, a thin layer of fat on the surface, the residue of decomposing gobies, may signal the presence of the prey and their predators. If there are no rocks or sunken

FIGURE 3.2
Large Boat of the Industrial Fishing and Shrimp Fleet Exploiting the Estuary

FIGURE 3.3
Part of the Estuary Industrial Fishing Fleet at Dock in Belém

ships in the area, nets can be placed in the water with relatively little danger of becoming entangled.

Once a fishing site is selected, the motor is turned off, and the boat is positioned so that the wind and/or tides will allow it to traverse the area where the gill net is stretched out (figure 3.4). Gill nets under 1,000 m length can be handled by two fishermen. One feeds the net into the water from the bow, while the second (and usually the more experienced) fisherman determines the depth to which the net will be allowed to sink. The number of floats left on the float-line controls the depth to which the net will sink.

The depth to which the gill net is allowed to sink depends on the characteristics of the bottom, such as whether it is rock or mud; the time of year; and the species being exploited. When the bottom is mud, which is the benthic habitat above which piramutaba are most often captured, fishermen first measure water depth with a weighted line to determine how deep to sink the gill net. Dourada, on the other hand, are mostly taken in mid- to surface waters. The most dangerous aspect of surface fishing is that nets can be cut when ships and boats pass. Because of this problem, estuarine fishermen exploiting open waters prefer to sink gill nets at least 6 m below the surface.

There are no environmental obstacles to fishing at night, although estuarine fishermen commonly work mostly during the day, especially in areas where

FIGURE 3.4
Gill-Net Fishing in the Estuary

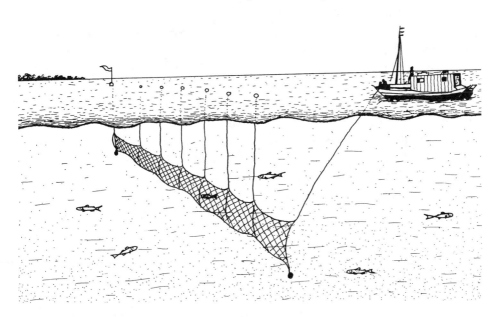

there is intense fishing activity. Fishermen worry that their nets may be cut and stolen at night. In areas where there is less fishing activity, such as along the coast of Amapá, the nets are left in the water day and night.

Estuarine gill nets are seldom used in a fixed position but rather drifted with the currents. The nets are stretched to the most perpendicular position possible in relation to the current. They are then allowed to drift downstream as far as 20 km. When used in a fixed position, gill nets are weighted with rocks or other types of anchors. This type of fishing is usually practiced in areas where drifting gill nets would get hung up on rocks. It is also restricted to the falling tide cycle, when waters are calmer.

The time that gill nets are left in the water corresponds roughly to tidal cycles, about five to six hours. Hauling in nets requires at least two or three people. One fisherman pulls the net aboard. A second helps, but his primary job is to remove any fish that are enmeshed. The third fisherman, when present, folds the net and rolls up the float-line. When smaller gill nets are used, the third fisherman is not necessary.

As the net is pulled aboard, fish are placed on the upper deck. Only after the net has been replaced in the water are the captured fish stored in the ice box. Boats without ice boxes place the fish in the hold to prevent spoilage in the sun. Such boats must then travel to port or sell their catches to a nearby ice boat. If they are far from an urban center or a boat with refrigeration facilities, they use salt to preserve their catches. This is especially common along the coast of the state of Amapá.

Most of the dourada and piraíba catch taken in the Amazon River, Rio Madeira, Rio Purus, and Rio Juruá is taken with what have now been called drifting deepwater gill nets (Goulding 1979, 1981; Rodríguez Fernández 1991). These are very similar but usually smaller than the gill nets used in the estuary (figure 3.5). Deepwater gill nets are drifted downstream at depths ranging from midwater to the bottom. Two fishermen usually work together in one canoe. The gill net is pulled aboard the canoe every one to four hours to remove the catch. In some cases, the net must be checked more regularly because highly voracious smaller catfishes (usually called candirú) of the families Cetopsidae and Trichyomycteridae attack the entangled catches. Candirú, capable of biting out sizable chunks of flesh, can destroy a catch.

Belém gill-net fishermen often move as far upstream as Santarém to exploit the Rio Amazonas during catfish migrations. In the 1970s and 1980s a few boats followed piramutaba and dourada schools to Tefé, 2,000 km upstream, in the region of the middle Rio Solimões, but today these fisheries are divided among several fishing fleets along the main river. Belém and Macapá boats move inland between May and November to capture catfish schools in the Rio Amazonas. Boat owners or managers have local informants along the main

FIGURE 3.5
Drifting Deepwater Gill Net Used in River Channels to Catch Large Catfish

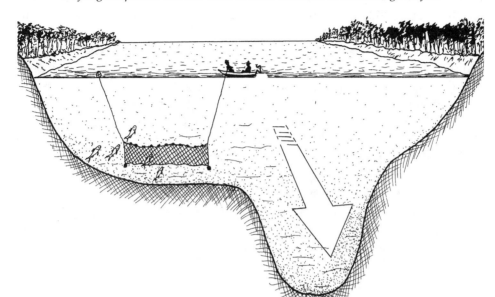

river who send messages by passenger boats or other means when catfish schools appear in their stretch of river. Piramutaba and dourada are spotted when the fish break the surface. These surfacings are usually very subtle, and only experienced residents or fishermen can spot them. Informants are rewarded with money, goods, or fish for their information.

TROTLINE FISHING

A trotline is a long line to which is attached a series of hooks suspended on shorter lines. One end of the trotline is fixed to some shore object, such as a bush or tree, or to a float. A weight at the other end carries the trotline to the bottom. In the estuary, trotlines are usually no more than about 65 m long, but longer trotlines, up to about 200 m, are used in Amazonian rivers to catch large catfish. These long trotlines are often stretched from the shore to the deepest parts of the channel.

In the estuary, trotlines are relatively unimportant compared to gill nets, as considerable work or extra expense is needed to obtain bait. Amuré gobies (*Gobioides* spp.) are the principal bait used to catch piramutaba (figure 3.6); they are never used for human consumption. There are fishermen who specialize in catching gobies and selling them to catfish operations. Most of these fishermen—"goby fishermen" or "cormorants" in local parlance—are either too young or too old to fish in the open waters of the estuary or sea. All that is needed to fish gobies is a canoe, a castnet, and a box to contain the catch. Goby fishermen usually work in groups. Choosing a shallow area during the low tide, they beach and tie up their canoes. Each fisherman then removes his clothes and, carrying a long stake and a floatable storage box, enters the water to a depth of up to 6 m. Shuffling their feet through the mud, they locate goby "houses," that is, the holes that these fish make and where they are commonly found. Each goby hole might contain four to five inhabitants. Once promising holes are located, the stakes are driven into the mud, and the storage box is tied to it. Holding on to his stake, a fisherman then dives to the bottom and covers the goby hole or holes with the castnet (which is not actually cast in this case). He then steps on the area above the holes or passes his hands over them, in order to scare the gobies out of hiding into the waiting net. The fish are then removed and deposited in the storage box. The process is repeated at each site. Because the storage box has holes or cracks

FIGURE 3.6
Goby Fishing in the Estuary

in it, water flows through it, and the gobies are thus kept alive until they are sold to other fishermen.

In estuarine locations where gobies are not available, mapará catfishes (*Hypophthalmus* spp., Hypophthalmidae) and shrimp are commonly used as bait. Mapará are purchased from fishermen exploiting the lower Rio Xingu near Cametá or the Baía de Marajó. Hoatzin (a bird), sloth, and boa constrictor meat are also occasionally employed as trotline bait. Inland fisheries use a wider variety of bait, most of which consists of species on which large catfishes are known to prey. Many fishermen believe that such fish as the matrichão (*Brycon* spp.) and jaraqui (*Semaprochilodus*), both of which are also commercial food fishes, are the best bait. Bait selection has yet to be tested statistically to see to what extent predators are attracted to certain species.

In the estuary, trotlines are placed and checked for catches during the changing of the tides, when water is most calm (figure 3.7). Fishing spots for trotlines are greatly limited by competition from gill-net fishermen. Trotline fishermen usually fish in areas with rocky or sandy bottoms. The weighted trotline is first placed in the water, followed by the floats and baited hooks. The current then drags the trotline until it is fully stretched and sunk. The hooks are only rebaited at the next changing of the tides, when the floats bring them to the surface.

FIGURE 3.7
Estuary Trotline

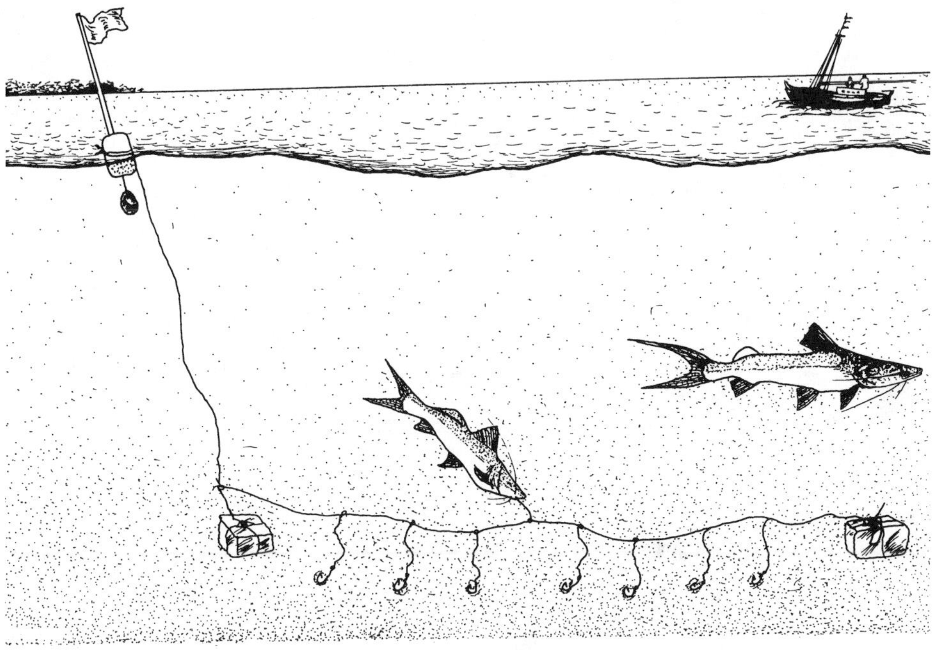

Large hooks and strong synthetic lines are now available throughout the Amazon. Hooks are sometimes manufactured locally from steel bars, but more often they are purchased. The two basic methods by which hooks are used to capture large river-channel catfishes are on trotlines and handlines. Trotlines are by far the more important, since handlines require the fishermen to be present, whereas trotlines can be left alone and merely checked periodically.

Trotlines used in river channels are either tied to a tree, shrub, or stake along the shore or to a floating object, such as a chunk of wood, a piece of Styrofoam, or a plastic container (figure 3.8). Both options necessitate the use of a weight to anchor the hooked end of the line to the bottom. Usually four to seven hooks are used when the trotline is sunken in the middle of the channel. When it is stretched near to shore, many more hooks may be used. The hooks are suspended on short lines 0.5–3.0 m in length. They are usually baited just before sunset and checked at daybreak. After a catfish is hooked, it remains relatively calm until a fisherman begins to pull it in; when it breaches the surface, it will turn and run. Experienced fishermen will be ready for this dangerous moment because other hooks may have been pulled aboard ahead of the one the catch

FIGURE 3.8
Trotline Used in River Channels of the Upper Amazon in the
Rio Caquetá Region of Colombia

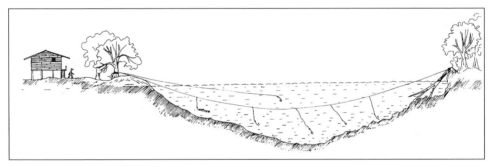

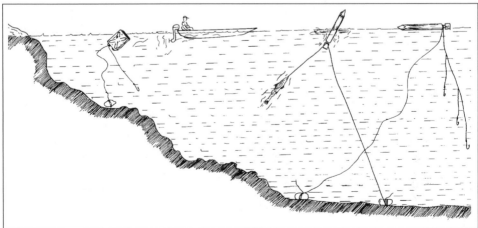

Source: Rodríguez Fernández 1991.

has taken, and the fish can pull these through a fisherman's hands. If a fisherman is accidentally hooked, a large catfish, or a catch of two or three on the same line, can even pull him overboard, where death, though not inevitable, is a real possibility.

CATFISH SEINES

The demand for piramutaba created by refrigeration companies in Belém led to the introduction of large beach seines especially adapted to capture these catfish (figure 3.9). This method, however, is now used mostly by Manaus fishermen exploiting the Rio Solimões, as it is effectively prohibited in the state of Pará. The catfish seine differs from counterparts used to catch smaller fish in the Amazon in that it has a larger mesh size, a heavier line, and a height of 45 m or more. Seines used to catch smaller fish usually measure no more than about 25 m in height.

When piramutaba are migrating upstream, seine fishermen locate submerged beaches over which the schools will pass. The 300–500 m seines are stretched as perpendicular as possible. When the school arrives in the beach area, the net is closed and dragged ashore. This method can capture up to thirty tons in one seining, which is often enough to fill a boat to its capacity.

FIGURE 3.9
Catfish Seine Used in Amazon River Channel

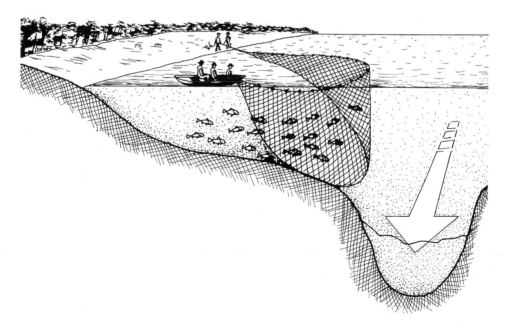

GILL-NET SEINES

The gill-net seine differs from the catfish seine in that is has larger mesh size and can be used either as a stationary gill net or as a seine. Its use is restricted mostly to beach areas where there are few obstructions, such as sunken wood, where the net might get tangled. The gill-net seine is used mostly to capture surubim and caparari catfishes (*Pseudoplatystoma* spp.) and the pirarara (*Phractocephalus hemiliopterus*).

HARPOONS AND SPEARS

Harpoons have long been used in the Amazon to capture a variety of large fishes. Though this type of fishing is still important for taking the large pirarucu (*Arapaima gigas*) in floodplain waters, it accounts for less than 1 percent of the commercial catfish catch in the central part of the Amazon Basin. Spears are used extensively, especially near rapids, in the Rio Caquetá region, where they account for about 75 percent of the total catfish catch (Muñoz Sosa 1993).

GAFF FISHERIES

Gaff fisheries in the Amazon are only known in the rapids of the upper Rio Madeira (figure 3.10). Most gaff fishing takes place at the Cachoeira de Teotônio just above Porto Velho. Gaff fishing at Teotônio is intense from December through February when dourada and babão are migrating upstream. The Teotônio rapids have a 7-m drop, between smooth water above and below the cataracts. From December through February, the Rio Madeira rises rapidly, and catfishes migrating upstream must fight their way along the left shore, where the current is still very strong but less overwhelming than in other parts of the cataract. Teotônio fishermen build platforms that allow them to perch above and thus gaff the upstream-migrating fish. Teotônio is the only known site in the central Amazon where large catfishes can be easily observed migrating upstream.

CASTNETS

Castnets are widely used in the Amazon for a variety of fisheries. Overall they are of more importance in subsistence fishing than to commercial fisheries.

FIGURE 3.10
Gaff Fisheries at the Cachoeira de Teotônio of the Upper Rio Madeira

The only place where castnets are regularly used to take large catfish for commercial sale is at the Cachoeira de Teotônio of the upper Rio Madeira and in some of the headwater areas, such as the Rio Caquetá (Goulding 1979, 1980; Rodríguez Fernández 1991). Teotônio fishermen perch themselves at various points in the cataracts on rocks from which they can cast their nets over the catfish as they fight their way through the rough waters.

TRAWLS AND INDUSTRIAL FISHERIES OF THE ESTUARY

The only gear of importance in industrial fisheries is the otter trawl (Castillo 1978), known as the Denmark or Portuguese trawl in Brazil. The tunnel part of the trawl measures about 45 m at the opening and is 75 m long (figure 3.11). Brazilian law has set the tunnel mesh size to at least 10 cm, though in the past estuarine operations used mesh as small as 5 cm. The boats are fully seaworthy, so they can exploit the open waters to the north and east of Marajó, the broad contact zone where the Rio Amazonas and the Rio Tocantins meet the ocean.

Trawl boats, fishing in pairs, rely on both experienced local fishermen and sonar devices to locate schools. Once a fish school is located, one of the trawl

FIGURE 3.11
Otter Trawl Used in Industrial Fisheries of the Estuary to Capture Piramutaba

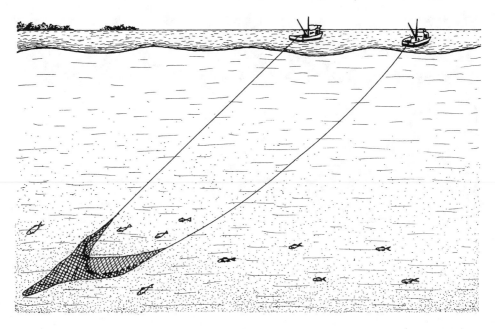

ropes on the boat carrying the net is transferred to the second ship. The two boats, keeping about 100 m apart, then drag the trawl net, sunk 20 to 40 m deep. If many fish are present the trawl can fill in less than thirty minutes. When fish are sparse, the net can be left in the water for the duration of the tidal cycle. Once the catch is brought aboard, it is spread out on the deck, and fish are sorted by size and species. In the past, all piramutaba smaller than about 1 kg were discarded. Now, however, with declining catches, smaller piramutaba are also being processed. Fishermen exploiting catfish take mostly piramutaba, but dourada and piraíba are also kept for sale. Fishermen admit that occasionally up to 80 percent of many trawl catches is not kept. These dead fish are discarded in nearby waters.

4

Catfish Yields and Value

The first general analysis of Amazonian fisheries was presented at the end of the last century (Veríssimo 1895). José Veríssimo was born and raised in Óbidos on the middle Rio Amazonas and later lived in Belém before moving south to Rio de Janeiro, where he eventually became one of Brazil's most famous literary and education scholars. An acute observer, Veríssimo divided Amazonian fisheries into two main categories: those targeting marine catfishes (*Arius parkeri*) and mullet in the estuary and those focusing on manatee and pirarucu (*Arapaima gigas*) in the interior. Veríssimo states that the large freshwater catfishes were exploited in the interior by small-scale fisheries during the migration season. The famous zoologist Emilio Goeldi, after whom the Goeldi Museum in Belém was named, mentions that freshwater catfish captured in the estuary were sold to the poorest classes in the city (Goeldi 1897). Belém fishermen, then, knew about the presence of large stocks of freshwater catfishes in the estuary as early as the last century.

For reasons that have yet to be clarified, there is a taboo in much of the

Central Amazon against eating catfish. This may have originated from interpretations of biblical passages prohibiting the consumption of scaleless fish. Until just recently, catfish were widely believed to cause or exacerbate a number of illnesses, ranging from skin inflammations to liver damage. Taboos are still common in the Amazon (Begossi and Braga, 1992; Smith, 1979, 1981), although there is no scientific evidence that eating catfish flesh causes health problems. Fishermen report that piraíba (*Brachyplatystoma filamentosum*) liver is toxic. If this is true it is probably caused by high levels of Vitamin A.

Because of the taboo, local consumption has been minimal in much of the Amazon. (In any case, the estuary and inland waters yield a variety and abundance of other fish stocks that can be exploited.) Petrere Jr. (1978b, 1985a) showed that less than 1 percent of the fish consumed in Manaus in 1976 was catfish. Data for the Iquitos, Peru, area indicate that only about 2 percent of the total catch of this region was made up of catfish (Barthem, Guerra, and Valderrama 1995). Whatever the reasons for the boycott, there has been little commercial value in catfish locally.

Historically, the situation in Belém has been strikingly different. The first catfish exploited in the estuary on a large scale was gurijuba, a marine species that was captured mostly in order to make glue, filters, and other products from its various parts. It has also been consumed as food since at least the last century. Freshwater species, however, are the preferred catfish in Belém. In 1994 approximately 25 percent of the fish consumed in the capital city was dourada and piramutaba (figure 4.1). First-class restaurants in Belém, however, rarely serve piramutaba and dourada and instead use piraíba in their catfish dishes.

ECONOMIC VALUE OF CATFISH EXPORTS

The economic importance of fish in the Amazon has long been recognized but there are still few data to quantify it. By 1981 estuarine fish and shrimp together represented the fifth most important category of products exported from the state of Pará, or a total value of about $13 million (CACEX–Banco do Brasil 1980). Piramutaba represented about 90 percent of the total value of the fish exported. In 1994 fish were the eleventh most important product exported from Pará, with a total value of about $3 million. At the national level, piramutaba captured in the Amazon estuary represented the third most important fish species exported from Brazil in 1986 and 1987, following tuna and snapper captured in offshore waters (Anonymous 1988). All these values are based on wholesale prices of about fifty cents per kilogram of fish. This is below the average international price for quality fish.

FIGURE 4.1
Dourada Being Sold at the Belém Fish Market

FIGURE 4.2
Value of Piramutaba Exports Since 1978

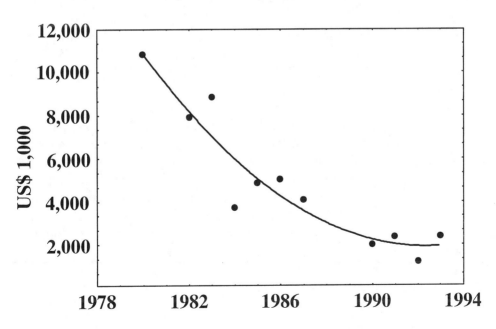

The most reliable data on large catfish are from exports (figure 4.2). In 1980 the state of Pará, Brazil, reported that it had exported $13 millon worth of fish; by 1990 this number had fallen to less than $1 million, because of reduced catches and fish size. In 1983 the state of Amazonas, Brazil, exported a reported $1.5 million worth of fish. These estimates are based on local, not international, prices. Large catfishes represent 80 to 100 percent of the fish exported annually from the Amazon since the early 1970s.

MARKET AND ECOLOGICAL DATA ON THE CATFISH FISHERIES

In the last century, Veríssimo (1895) emphasized how important it was to collect statistical information on the fisheries of the Amazon, as these data would be needed in order to set up management programs. Despite his urging, however, the first data of any merit on estuarine fisheries only began to be collected in the late 1970s. Castillo (1978), Dias-Neto and Pontes (1982), Furtado (1981, 1987), and Loureiro (1985) described the gear being used and the socioeconomic conditions of the fishermen operating in the estuary. Petrere Jr. (1978a, 1978b, 1985) recorded detailed information on the Manaus market in the last half of the 1970s, though data from refrigeration companies were not included in the analyses; his data showed that dourada and piramutaba were not popular food fishes in Manaus. Farther downriver, at Itacoatiara, on the Rio Amazonas, Smith (1979, 1981) also showed that these catfishes were not heavily exploited for local consumption. Catfish catches were registered in the upper Rio Madeira region between 1977 and 1979, and most of the catch was exported to southern Brazil for lack of a local market (Goulding 1979, 1981). Boischio (1992) reviewed Porto Velho market data between 1984 and 1989, at which time dourada represented about 8 percent of the catch sold in Rondonia's capital.

Both the present authors, as employees of the Goeldi Museum, set up data-collecting programs in the Belém market in the early 1980s in order to learn more about catfish ecology (Barthem 1985; Barthem, Ribeiro, and Petrere Jr. 1991). Barthem also established a large-scale database on various aspects of estuarine ecology that continues to this day (Barthem and Schwassmann 1994).

The first database on large catfish ecology in inland waters contains information on the upper Rio Madeira region (Goulding 1979, 1981). It was later expanded to include the Rio Amazonas, Rio Solimões, Rio Purus, and Rio Juruá in various years in the 1980s, the results of which will be reported herein. Finally, as part of the present project, Barthem at the Goeldi Museum brought together market and refrigeration plant data for the 1990s from Leticia, Tefé, Lábrea, Manaus, Itacoatiara, Parintins, Santarém, and Belém (figures 4.3 and 4.4).

FIGURE 4.3
Market Sites Where Catfish Data Have Been Collected Since the 1970s

FIGURE 4.4
Catfish Catches Purchased by Refrigeration Plants in Years for Which Data Are Available

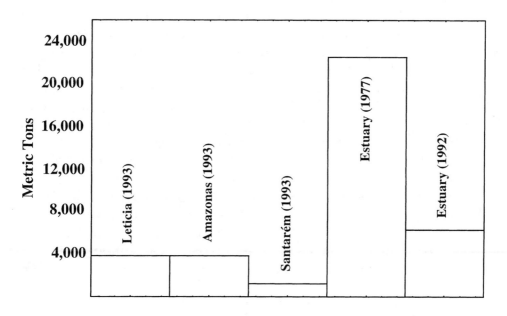

PIRAMUTABA FISHERIES IN THE ESTUARY

Until the late 1960s Amazonian fisheries were relatively small-scale operations. The human population of the region was minimal, and most of the commercial catch was destined for small urban centers. In 1960 Manaus and Belém, the largest cities, each had populations of less than 300,000. Fish was sold either fresh or salted, and there were no large-scale storage facilities.

In the 1960s, however, the Brazilian government began to offer incentives to increase the size of fishing fleets in the Amazon and to modernize equipment, especially in the estuarine region. Most attention was initially focused on the estuary because its productivity was known to be high (Britto et al. 1975). By 1968 refrigeration companies began to build plants in the municipality of Belém, planning to buy, process, and store fish for national and international markets (Penner 1980).

Local fishermen made it known that there were large, unexploited stocks of piramutaba, the species they believed to be the most abundant. It was considered a second- or third-class food fish in Belém, but refrigeration companies found the species to be more acceptable abroad, especially in the United States, but also in Germany, Japan, Holland, and Nigeria. Piramutaba was also found to freeze well. Furthermore, export fisheries faced no competition from local markets.

Refrigeration plants built in the Belém area opened the way for the industrialization of estuarine fisheries. By 1972 the Brazilian government backed loans for the construction of larger and more efficient boats, the majority of which were made of steel, and the purchase of trawl seines. Other government incentives included tax breaks and relaxation of import restrictions on equipment (Britto et al. 1975; SUDEPE 1979; Dias-Neto, Damasceno, and Pontes 1985).

Estuarine fisheries are now divided between industrial and small-scale operations. Industrial fisheries are fairly homogeneous and mostly exploit piramutaba and shrimp. Between 1972 and 1978 the industrial fisheries aimed at export markets accounted for about 70 percent of the average annual captures of piramutaba (Dias-Neto and Mesquita 1988). The total capture of all fish by the industrial operations was actually much greater, as rejected catches from trawls alone are estimated to have averaged more than 50 percent of total catches (Castillo 1978). This waste continues to this day.

Export fisheries based on the Amazon estuary boomed during the 1970s. The maximum catch recorded to date was 28,000 tons; it was taken in 1977 (figure 4.5). By 1988, however, piramutaba catches fell drastically, to half the 1977 catch, and overexploitation was suspected to account for the drop. Stocks continue to be heavily exploited, though annual catches have not exceeded 10,000 tons since 1988.

FIGURE 4.5

Annual Catch of Piramutaba by Industrial Fishing Fleets Based in the Amazon Estuary

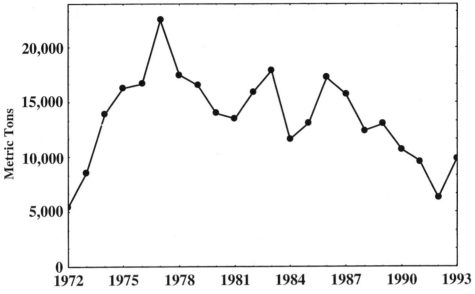

COLOMBIA

Only 120 km of the Amazon River passes through Colombian territory. Leticia is Colombia's port on the Amazon. The town possesses no roads to other major Colombian cities, and all transport is done by air or boat. Since the early 1970s Colombians have used the port to export catfish to Bogotá (Bayley 1981). Peruvian, Brazilian, and Colombian fishermen have been involved in these fisheries, and an area from about Tefé, on the middle Rio Solimões, to Iquitos is exploited. Bayley (1981) estimated that 8,000–10,000 tons of catfish were exported annually to Bogotá in the 1970s. At that time, catfish were salted. Today, Leticia has more than a dozen refrigeration companies, and frozen fish is transported by air to Bogotá. In 1993 at least 6,000 tons of catfish were exported from Leticia to Bogotá (figure 4.6). At present most of the catch consists of dourada.

AMAZONAS, BRAZIL

The state of Amazonas in Brazil has refrigeration plants that freeze fish in Manaus, Itacoatiara, Manacapuru, Iranduba, Lábrea, and Parintins. The largest plants are in Manaus and Iranduba. According to data supplied by

FIGURE 4.6

Catfish Catch Purchased by Refrigeration Companies in Leticia, Colombia,
the Amazonas State of Brazil, and Santarém in 1993

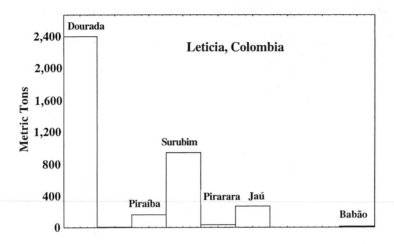

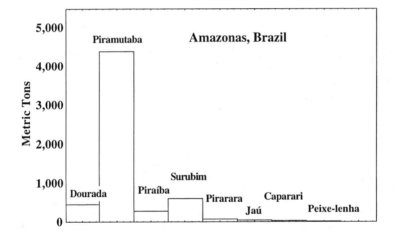

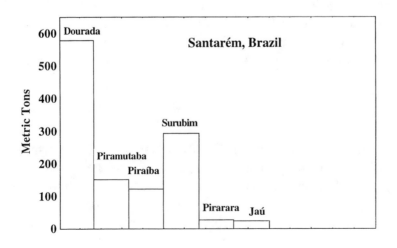

Brazil's Ministry of Agriculture, the total catfish catch processed in the state of Amazonas in 1993 was at least 5,400 tons, or nearly equal to that reported as being exported from Leticia to Bogotá. Most of the fish exported from the state of Amazonas is barged in freezer containers to Belém and then shipped or trucked to other countries and southern Brazil. Some is also exported by jet from Manaus to the United States and southern Brazil.

PARÁ, BRAZIL

In the state of Pará, upstream of the estuary, there are refrigeration plants that freeze catfish in Santarém and Óbidos. Catfish-export companies have been operating in both cities since the early 1980s. Santarém is by far the most important catfish market along the Rio Amazonas upriver of the estuary. In 1993 approximately 2,500 tons of catfish were processed in Santarém for export.

5

Migration and Reproduction

Humans have known about and exploited animal migrations at least as long as we have been *Homo sapiens*. It is only recently, however, that we have begun to take steps to protect migratory animals, and these efforts become more difficult each year because of the large-scale modification of habitats. Migratory fish are by far the most important food fish species exploited in the Amazon, and it is vital that we understand as much as possible about their movements. To date, only one large river has been dammed in the Amazon. Pollution has not been a serious problem along the main stem. Mercury contamination from gold-mining operations is a concern in some of the tributaries, but we still have no information on how this is affecting fish populations in general (but see Boischio 1995).

Discussions of migration can get bogged down in theoretical arguments about what exactly the word means. The main problem arises because animals make many different kinds of movements, and we understand relatively little about most species. Reviews of what is known about fish migrations in the oceans and inland waters make it apparent that the least is known about tropical fishes (e.g., Baker 1978; Leggett 1977, 1985; Lowe-McConnell 1975, 1977, 1979, 1984, 1987; McCleave 1985; McDowall 1988; Northcote 1985; Smith 1985). In the tropics, however, more is known about South American rivers than any others (Lowe-McConnell 1987). Within South America the Amazon Basin is the least known, and it also appears to have the greatest diversity of fish migrations.

A rigid definition of migration does not seem useful to us, and we will not attempt one here. All the large catfishes we discuss would be considered migratory by almost any textbook definition: they make regular movements from one habitat or place to another during the course of the year or at various parts of their life cycles. The issue becomes more complicated when an attempt is made to classify the various types of fish migrations. Fisheries biologists generally use the terms *diadromous, anadromous, catadromous,* and *potamodromous* to describe the basic types of migrations (Myers 1949; McDowall 1988). All the species studied herein would be considered potamodromous because they live strictly in freshwater. However, the migratory patterns of at least three catfish species—dourada, piramutaba, and babão—are reminiscent of diadromous patterns, that is, involving migration between the sea and freshwaters. Unlike diadromous species, though, Amazon freshwater catfish stop at the estuary and do not enter the salt water of the ocean. There is no specific term for freshwater fish that migrate to and from estuaries, although the distances covered by some of the Amazonian species make them reminiscent of diadromous animals.

The functional purposes of fish migrations are not as obvious as they might at first seem to be. The main problem lies in lack of data on the dynamics of the physical, biological, and historical factors that have affected populations. It does seem reasonable to believe, however, that the redistribution of part or all of a population in time and space can lead to all or some combination of the following: increased growth rates, decreased mortality, and increased reproduction.

THE ABSENCE OF DIADROMOUS SPECIES IN THE AMAZON

The most striking fact about migratory fishes in the Amazon is that diadromous (freshwater-saltwater migrations or vice versa) species are missing. The bullsharks and sawfishes that travel far up the Amazon River are wanderers, and it is certain that their life cycles do not depend on a freshwater phase; only in the broadest sense would anyone consider them to be diadromous fishes. Furthermore, they do not form schools when moving up the Amazon. It is possible that herring (*Pellona* spp.) and perhaps some croaker species (*Plagioscion* spp.) of the lower Amazon migrate between freshwater and salt or brackish water, but their numbers must be relatively small because these movements are not obvious to fishermen. If they do take place, they are confined to the estuary, as otherwise they would almost certainly be familiar to fishermen exploiting the inland waters.

There are about 180 known diadromous fish species in the world. The majority of them are found in temperate latitudes. The most famous and best-studied are salmon, although many other families are involved as well (McDowall 1988). At least twenty fish families that have species known to be diadromous in other parts of the world are found in the Amazon Basin and/or the Atlantic adjacent to its eastern limits. It is important to note, however, that none of these families has representatives that make long migrations on the scale associated with salmon, *Anguilla* eels, and some other temperate-latitude groups. Most of the tropical species are associated with inland movements that involve only the lower courses of rivers and estuaries. It is thus possible that the Amazon Basin does not have obligatory diadromous species because the main families from which these species evolved are not found in the trop-ical Atlantic. On the other hand, the Amazon Basin has at least 50 species whose relatives are mostly marine. Nearly all, if not all, of these species evolved to conduct their lives entirely in freshwater.

It could be argued that the rich predatory fish fauna of the Amazon has pre-vented the evolution of diadromous species in the region, although there is probably no way to test this hypothesis. The Amazon has the richest freshwa-ter fish fauna in the world, and it is possible that diadromous species cannot establish themselves in waters dominated by diverse communities occupying what are supposedly most if not all of the major niches available. Again, this may have been what happened, but it is probably impossible to test, short of large-scale introductions of diadromous species from other continental regions, which we do not recommend.

CHARACIN MIGRATIONS OUTSIDE THE AMAZON BASIN

The evolutionary ecology of migration is best approached from a broad per-spective so that comparisons can be made in an attempt to understand life-cycle strategies. This discussion is restricted mostly to characins, as the most is known about them (see also Lowe-McConnell 1975, 1979, 1987; Petrere Jr. 1985b; Vazzoler and Menezes 1992; Menezes and Vazzoler 1992).

South America's three great river systems are the Amazon, the Paraguay-Paraná, and the Orinoco. The Amazon lies between the other two. The fish fau-nas of all three systems were derived from basically the same ancestors after the separation of Africa and South America. Fish migrations were first studied in the upper Rio Paraná system in Brazil in the 1950s (Godoy 1959, 1967, 1975). The middle Paraná was later investigated by Argentineans in the 1960s (Bonetto and Pignalberi 1964; Bonetto, Pignalberi, and Yuan 1971). The Paraná is the only river system in South America where large-scale tagging experiments have been made successfully.

Most fish migration information from southern South America focuses on curimatá (*Prochilodus* spp.), although other species have been tagged as well. Fish migrations in the Rio Mogi Guassu of the upper Paraná system were easily detected at rapids, and even more so after hydroelectric barriers were constructed. Tagging experiments showed that curimatá (*Prochilodus scrofa*) form large schools and migrate upstream on an annual basis to spawn in headwater regions, usually near or above rapids. Subsequent to spawning, the fish then migrate about 600 km downstream to their main feeding habitats. The annual migratory cycle in the upper Paraná involves a 1,200-km round-trip. Spawning takes place during the floods. Experiments showed that curimatá migrate upstream at an average of 5–8 km/day, but less rapidly downstream, covering only about 3.5 km/day. The tagging data showed that fish populations in the upper Paraná were separated from the middle and lower reaches of the system in Argentina.

During the 1960s Argentineans tagged twenty-five fish species in the middle and lower Paraná region (Bonetto and Pignalberi 1964; Bonetto, Pignalberi, and Yuan 1971), concentrating the most effort on *Prochilodus platensis*. These experiments showed that various populations in the middle Paraná and Uruguay systems move upstream to spawn and downstream to feed in the lower reaches. The researchers calculated upstream migrations of *Prochilodus platensis* to be about 8.7 km/day and downstream movements to be about 5 km/day. The annual round-trip was about 1,300 km.

The Rio Paraguay is a tributary of the middle Paraná in the region of the Gran Chaco, a large swampy area. The Rio Pilcomayo is a tributary of the Rio Paraguay, and its headwaters flow from the Andes. Bayley (1970, 1973) showed that at least five characin and one catfish species ascend the Rio Pilcomayo to spawn in the Andean foothills. There is almost no floodplain in this region. The migratory schools first arrive in May and June. Spawning takes place a day after the first heavy floods. By November and December, when the main floods come, the fish descend to the swampy lower reaches of the river. The migratory cycle involves an 800-km round-trip.

The Rupununi is a large savanna region in Guyana that is drained by the Essequibo. When rivers begin to rise in May and June, large characins move upriver and into streams penetrating the surrounding savannas. These species include the large *Myleus pacu*, a large pacu; predatory dogtooth characins

(*Hydrolycus*); and characin-pike (*Boulengerella*). Also present was *Prochilodus*. During the floods, the Rupununi savannas are inundated 1–2 m, and the fish move into these habitats to spawn (Lowe-McConnell 1964, 1987). When waters subside after the rains, the fish return to the river channels or get trapped in pools.

Massive upstream fish migrations have been observed in the Orinoco system, but they have not been studied as well there as in the Amazon (Novoa 1989). During the high-water months, July to September, huge schools of detritivores of the genus *Semaprochilodus* move out of the floodplains and into the river channels. They then move upstream and reportedly look for spawning habitats. Another detritivore, *Prochilodus mariae*, is said to show two annual movements. During the dry season, schools move upstream, but sexually mature (ripe) fish are not present. At the beginning of the floods, ripe fish move upstream for spawning. Large schools of cachama (*Colossoma macropomum*) and morocoto (*Piaractus brachypomus*) are said to move upstream during the dry season and back down with the rains (Novoa 1989; Taphorn 1992).

FISH MIGRATIONS IN THE RIO MADEIRA BASIN

The first models for Amazonian fish migrations were based on field observations and fisheries data from the middle and upper Rio Madeira (Goulding 1979, 1980, 1981; Goulding and Carvalho 1982). Ecologically this region is part of the Central Amazon. It is easier to observe fish migrations in the Rio Madeira than in the Amazon River because the tributary is considerably smaller and only a single channel is present in most of the middle and upper reaches. Finally, just above Porto Velho, 800 km upstream, there are a series of cataracts where fish movements can be easily detected at various times of the year.

The Rio Madeira model suggested that fish migration patterns in the Central Amazon were considerably different from those reported for the Paraná-Paraguay, Rupununi, and Orinoco systems. Approximately thirty species of characins were identified as seasonally migratory in the upper Rio Madeira. All the species live in both the main river and its tributaries, although there are considerable differences in seasonal and size-class distributions. The common denominator among the species is that they all spawn in the muddy water of the Rio Madeira. Depending on the species, spawning takes place between the beginning and the middle of the annual floods. Populations residing in the tributaries at the beginning of the floods migrate downstream in large schools to spawn in the Rio Madeira. Populations living in floodplain waters of the Rio Madeira migrate to the main channel or at least to invading muddy water. Subsequent to spawning, the fish then migrate to the flood-plains of the tributaries or to the Rio Madeira floodplain. The fish then disperse in flooded forests, where they then spent four to five months feeding.

After the peak of the annual floods, a second type of migration takes place. Large schools descend the clearwater and blackwater tributaries and then migrate upstream in the Rio Madeira. These fish then enter another tributary farther upstream than the one they had left. The total distance of these so-called dispersal migrations does not seem to be more than about 300–400 km and is often less than 100 km, although tagging experiments are necessary to test this observation. A third type of migration is apparent during the low-water period, when most species are found in large schools in the Rio Madeira. Near the lowest water point, there are intense upstream migrations of nearly all species. Throughout the Amazon, this type of upstream movement is referred to as the *piracema*. Ecologically it is possible that the *piracema* is a continuation of the dispersal migrations that begin as soon as water level begins to drop rapidly.

No larval fish were captured in the Rio Madeira channel, but it was hypothesized that they are carried downstream before finding their way into the main river's floodplain. The dispersal and *piracema* migrations mentioned above for adult fish would spatially counterbalance the downstream displacement of larvae. Experimental fishing showed that larvae and young fish of the migratory characins were missing from clearwater and blackwater tributaries but abundant in floodplain habitats of the Rio Madeira. Young fish require microorganisms in their diets, and these foods are much more abundant in muddy river floodplain waterbodies than in the clearwater and blackwater tributaries. It was thus hypothesized that spawning in muddy water was mainly an adaptation to place larvae in or near the most productive habitats for young fish.

FISH MIGRATIONS IN THE LOWER RIO NEGRO

The lower Rio Negro has been the region in the Amazon most intensively studied for characin migrations. Although migratory characins of the genus *Brycon* have been studied in the Rio Negro (Borges 1986), the most attention has been given to jaraqui (*Semaprochilodus taeniura* and *theroponura*), which are detritivorous fishes of the characin family, Prochilodontidae (Ribeiro 1983, 1984, 1990; Ribeiro and Petrere Jr. 1990; Vazzoler, Amadio, and Caraciolo-Malta 1989a, 1989b; Vazzoler and Amadio 1990; Vazzoler and Menezes 1992; Menezes and Vazzoler 1992). Jaraqui have been one of the most important food fishes in the Central Amazon since the early 1970s.

Rio Negro jaraqui undertake two annual migrations, one for spawning at the beginning of the floods and the other for dispersal just after the peak of the high-water season. During spawning runs jaraqui move down the Rio Negro to breed in the muddy Amazon River, after which they return to the tributary. After the peak of the floods, they again move down the Rio Negro but this time migrate upstream in the Amazon River until they enter another tributary or adjacent floodplain area. During the falling-water period, first-year fish (but not larvae) and adults are "recruited" into the Rio Negro from populations moving up the Amazon River. As was the case in the Rio Madeira, this behavior counterbalances the downstream displacement of newborn in the main river. Sampling showed that jaraqui larvae were absent from the Rio Negro but abundant in the floodplain waters of muddy rivers such as the Amazon and Rio Madeira (Ribeiro 1983; Bayley 1983; Ribeiro and Petrere Jr. 1990; Goulding, Carvalho, and Ferreira 1988).

FISH MIGRATIONS IN THE LOWER RIO TOCANTINS

Carvalho and Merona (1986) examined the migratory patterns of mapará catfish (*Hypophthalmus marginatus*) and curimatá (*Prochilodus nigricans*) in the Rio Tocantins. Their study was based on fisheries data taken before the Tucuruí dam was closed in 1984. Fisheries data indicated that mapará in the lower part of the river migrated as far as the first rapids, 270 km upstream, the site where the Tucuruí dam was located. Spawning reportedly took place at the beginning of the floods, and it was thought that larvae descended to the lower reaches where more feeding habitat was available. Our own collections have revealed that mapará larvae and young are present in the upper parts of the estuary.

The curimatá in the Rio Tocantins are evidently not part of the Central Amazon population. Rio Tocantins curimatá populations spend their entire lives within that river basin. Unlike mapará catfish, however, curimatá migrated far upstream of the first rapids (Ribeiro, Petrere Jr., and Juras 1995).

PIRAMUTABA MIGRATIONS IN THE AMAZON

Tagging and Observing Piramutaba

The booming industrial fisheries of the 1970s made it obvious that piramutaba was very abundant in the Amazon estuary. Information from local fishermen also made it clear that the species migrated upstream. The Faculty of the Agronomical Sciences of Pará (FCAP), with financing from the Superintendency of the Development of the Amazon (SUDAM), contracted the services of Manuel Pereira de Godoy, one of the pioneers in fish tagging in southern Brazil, to study piramutaba in the late 1970s. Godoy tagged over nine thousand piramutaba in the Amazon estuary in 1978. Less than 1 percent (0.67%) of the fish tagged were recaptured (or reported) either from experimental fishing (weirs) or commercial operations. All recaptures were also from the same area where the fish were initially tagged. No hypothesis could be presented based on these initial experiments (Godoy 1979).

Piramutaba are usually very difficult to detect in the muddy waters where the species is mostly found. During migrations, piramutaba rarely come to the surface in either the estuary or inland rivers. It is thus difficult if not impossible to follow schools based on visual observations alone. Fishermen, however, spot an occasional individual surfacing, and experience has taught them that this signals the presence of a school below. Piramutaba schools are also known to come to the surface to feed on prey, and the second author has observed this in the Rio Madeira. Sonar might prove useful to follow schools, but to date this method has not been attempted for lack of a meaningful model to conceptualize long-distance movements.

Fisheries Indicating the Presence of Piramutaba

Fishermen's reports make it clear that piramutaba have been exploited on a regular basis from the estuary to at least Leticia, Colombia, a distance of about 3,500 km (Barthem 1990a, 1990b). Pucallpa market data also show that piramutaba are captured in the Rio Ucayali, Peru, at least 4,500 km upstream, and in the Rio Caquetá, Colombia, 3,300–3,800 km upstream (Barthem, Guerra, and Valderrama 1995; Arboleda 1984; Muñoz Sosa 1993). A popular postcard sold in Porto Velho, Rondonia, in the 1970s showed large quantities of piramutaba being salted at the Cachoeira do Teotônio of the upper Rio Madeira, some 3,100 km upstream. There is thus persuasive evidence that the species is common as far upstream as the pre-Andean plains (at an elevation of more than 400 m) in Peru and Colombia. We are uncertain whether piramutaba are present in Bolivia above the Rio Madeira rapids.

Geographical Distribution of Piramutaba Size Classes

The geographical distribution of piramutaba size classes appears to be a clear indicator of migratory patterns. To compare size classes statistically, length measurements of 38,000 fish were taken and analyzed from four main areas of the Amazon River (estuary, central Amazon, upper Rio Madeira, and western Amazon). Most of the fish measured were captured in commercial operations with drifting deepwater gill nets. Gill nets capture fish selectively. The mesh sizes used by fishermen in the Brazilian Amazon for piramutaba are most efficient for size classes around 45 cm length. Over 95 percent of the commercial catch of piramutaba taken by the nonindustrial fleet consists of preadult or adult fish over 36 cm (figure 5.1). Only industrial fisheries in the estuary exploit smaller size classes.

To detect the presence of small size classes in areas and habitats not exploited by commercial operations, experimental fishing with gill nets and a trawl seine was employed in the estuary and at various points along the Amazon River. Only fish migrating upstream can be captured with drifting deepwater gill nets, thus downstream movements, if they take place, would not be detected with this method. As we suggest later, however, these movements might possibly take place during periods of the year when catches are minimal.

As part of other projects, we also sampled about twenty-five different rivers in the Amazon for fish populations. These collections clearly revealed that young piramutaba do not use floodplains as nursery habitats, as not even one specimen was collected (see, e.g., Barthem 1984, 1987).

Size-class data for piramutaba were obtained for the estuary, lower Rio Amazonas, the Manaus region of the Amazon River, Tefé, and Leticia. These data show that large size classes of piramutaba are found from the estuary to the Colombian-Peruvian border. Experimental fishing data revealed that very young piramutaba (less than 4 cm) are present in the estuary and Amazon River channel to at least as far as Tefé, 2300 km upstream. Intermediate size classes (5–15 cm) appear to be restricted mostly to the estuary.

Migratory Patterns of Preadults and Adults

Most of the piramutaba captured while migrating upstream in the Amazon River are preadult and adult fish. Migration of preadults and adults was verified by data collected from both commercial and experimental fishing (figure 5.2). During most of the high-water period of the Rio Amazonas, or from about January to May, there is no known upstream migration of piramutaba. At this time of year, the larger size classes spread out in the huge area of freshwater that dominates the estuary. This is corroborated by the correspondingly large area exploited by commercial fishermen at this time of year. The large amount of

FIGURE 5.1
*Frequency Distribution of Piramutaba Size Classes Along
the Amazon River and in the Estuary*

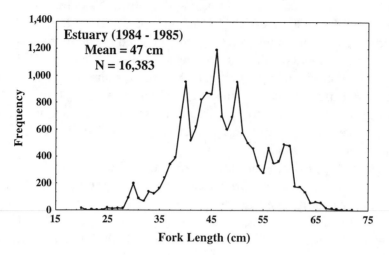

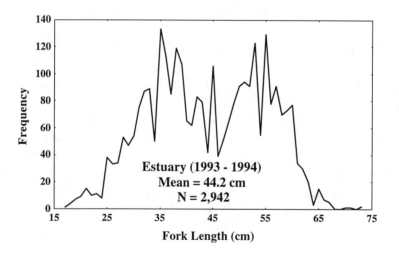

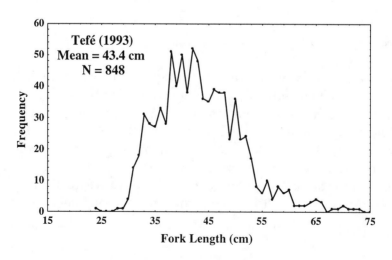

FIGURE 5.2
Monthly Captures of Piramutaba

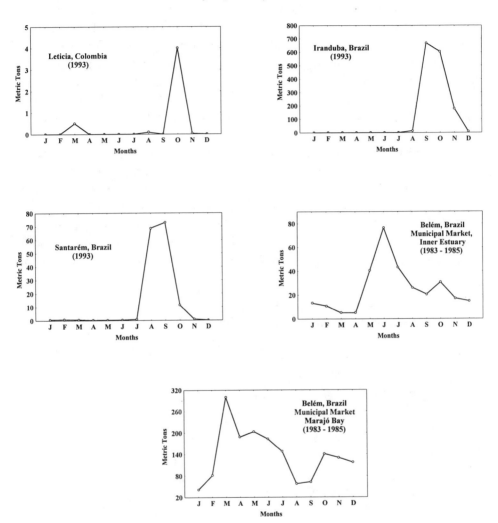

habitat offered and the intense primary production (algae) taking place provide huge quantities of food for the prey on which piramutaba feed (see chap. 6).

The southern part of the Amazon estuary, or the Baía de Marajó, is invaded by salt water as early as May, when the Rio Tocantins begins to fall. When this happens, piramutaba schools begin to move slowly toward the interior of the estuary to escape the brackish water. Where the dual tidal current is replaced by the unidirectional Rio Amazonas, piramutaba schools begin to migrate rapidly upstream. The first migratory schools of piramutaba in the lower Rio Amazonas appear in June. Based on fisheries data, the schools apparently originate in and then leave the estuary until at least October and perhaps November, but it is unclear whether they all continue to migrate upstream, at least past Santarém. In 1993, however, we noted that large schools passed Santarém, 880 km upstream, in August and September; peak catches for Manaus, 1,650 km upstream, were recorded in September and October; and at Leticia, 3,300 km upstream, peak catches were taken in October. Upper Rio Madeira fishermen report that piramutaba schools only reach the Teotônio rapids every five years or so, and then in the months of September or October. Fishermen believe that only in very low water years do piramutaba schools reach as far the upper Rio Madeira.

Based on the fisheries data outlined above, we believe that piramutaba schools take approximately five months to migrate from the estuary to the upper Amazon, a distance of about 3,300 km (figure 5.3). Upriver swimming speed appears to be about 22 km/day. The movements of piramutaba schools that we observed in the lower Amazon River region suggested an upriver swimming speed of 18–26 km/day. Most of the speeds reported for other South American fishes are less than this, although there are species with com-

FIGURE 5.3
Hypothesized Spawning (ellipse) and Nursery (box) Area of Piramutaba

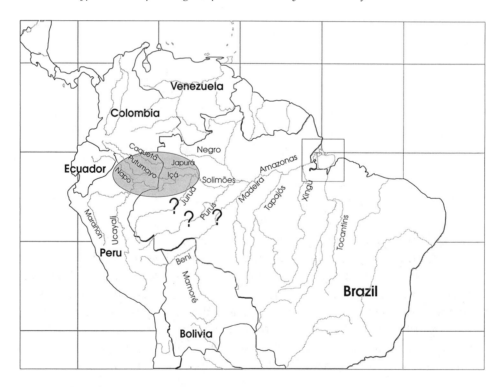

parable ascents on this continent and elsewhere in the tropics (Godoy 1967; Ribeiro 1983; Lowe-McConnell 1987).

A return migration of preadults and/or adults to the estuary from the upper Amazon is more problematic to prove because no fisheries or experimental data show that it takes place. Fish swimming downstream rarely get entangled in gill nets. Furthermore, during the floods Amazon River currents are much stronger, and returning fish from the Brazilian-Peruvian-Colombian border region would only need about ten to fifteen days to reach the estuary. Given the long distances covered and the swollen waters of the main stem, the chances of perceiving, let alone catching, these fish are minimal. Catch data, however, strongly suggest that the size classes that largely disappear from, or become rarer in, the estuary are present after January, and we believe the larger size classes captured after January are made up of fish that have returned from several thousand kilometers upstream.

Reproduction

Neither fishermen nor our own experimental fishing reveal anything about the exact spawning sites of piramutaba. We still do not have any direct evidence of spawning in the southern muddy water tributaries (Madeira, Juruá, and Purus), although piramutaba schools are known to enter these rivers. Relatively large numbers of sexually mature piramutaba are thus far only known for the Rio Caquetá region of Colombia (Arboleda 1984; Muñoz Sosa 1993). Market data presented by SUDEPE (1980) for Tabatinga at the Brazilian/Colombian border indicated that 5 percent of 298 piramutaba specimens examined between January and March were sexually mature. These fish, however, were not examined by biologists, thus we cannot be certain that these data are reliable. Based on a growth curve, we estimate that piramutaba spawn at about three years of age (figure 5.4).

The area near Tefé, about 2,300 km upstream, was the location closest to the estuary where a fully ripe piramutaba specimen was collected. This specimen was taken in August 1993 by the first author and is now in the fish collection of the Goeldi Museum in Belém (figure 5.5). Considering that ripe piramutaba have only been found far upstream and that the estuary has been heavily exploited for the species for over twenty years but no sexually mature individuals have been captured or reliably reported, it seems safe to assume that spawning only takes place in the western Amazon. This region probably involves the Amazon River and its main muddy tributaries, including the Rio Madeira.

FIGURE 5.4
Growth Curve of Sexual Maturity of Piramutaba (box)

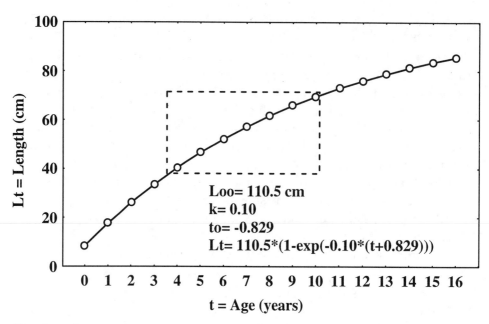

Based on the growth curve and four sexually mature individuals that were measured between 42 and 64 cm, we believe that piramutaba spawn after three years of age. The box indicates the size range of sexually mature fish that have thus far been found.

Data based on Barthem 1990b.

FIGURE 5.5
Ripe Female Piramutaba Captured about 2,300 km Up the Amazon River, Near Tefé

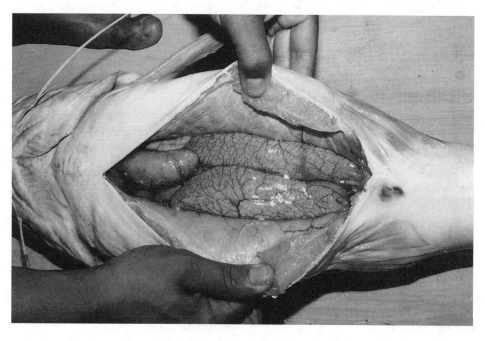

Downstream Migration of Larvae

To date, no one has captured piramutaba larvae less than 10 mm in length. In view of the fact that sexually mature individuals have only been captured in the western Amazon, it seems probable that piramutaba larvae remain in the general area where they are born for at least one week. We assume that they live on their yolk sacs during the first week of life.

Experimental fishing by the first author with an otter trawl (5 mm mesh at cod end) sunk to the bottom of the river channel of the Rio Solimões near Tefé and Rio Amazonas near the estuary captured young piramutaba measuring 13–30 mm in length (figure 5.6). Barletta (1995) also reported capturing comparably sized piramutaba in the Rio Amazonas near Manaus. In the estuary, small piramutaba less than 30 mm have only been found in water with very low or no salinity (figure 5.7) (Barthem 1985, 1990b). Based on comparisons with catfish species whose larval growth rates have been studied (see, e.g., Burr and Mayden 1982), these fish could not have been more than about two weeks old. Very young piramutaba were captured during both the high- and low-water seasons. Analyses of stomach contents revealed that these young catfish feed on phytoplankton, zooplankton, shrimp, and insects in the Amazon River channel (Barthem 1990b). We hypothesize that the downstream migration of young piramutaba involves stops, or at least delays, for feeding purposes.

FIGURE 5.6
Size Classes of Young Piramutaba Captured in Amazon River Channel Near Estuary

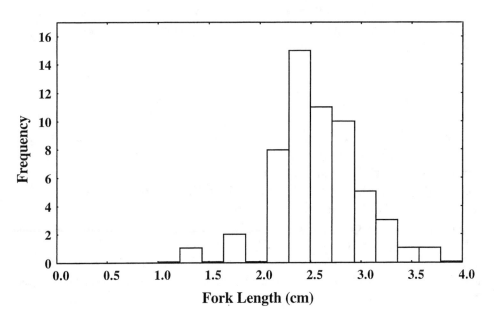

FIGURE 5.7

Catch of Piramutaba per Hour of Experimental Fishing in Relation to Water Conductivity

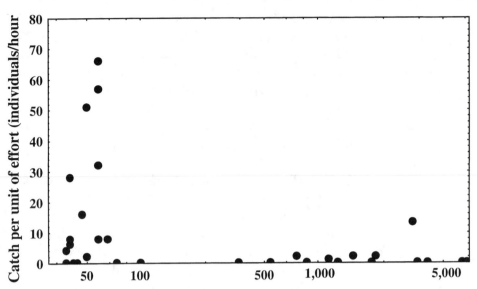

The current speed of the Amazon River ranges between 8 and 11 km/hour. Piramutaba born in the western Amazon could reach the estuary in thirteen to twenty days, even with brief daily delays for feeding. At this rate, larval fish would not be longer than 50 mm before reaching the estuary. Young piramutaba captured in the lower Rio Amazonas just downriver of the Rio Xingu were 13–36 mm in length (Barthem 1990b). This strongly suggests that young piramutaba take no longer than one month at most to reach the estuary from the western Amazon area where they are born.

Seasonal Movements of Juveniles in the Lower Amazon River

Other than the long-distance migrations outlined above, piramutaba also make seasonal movements that are confined to the estuary or lower Rio Amazonas. These movements were detected by experimental fishing (Barthem 1990b). During the first months of life in the estuary, piramutaba juveniles spread out in the open waters, where they live mostly on the bottom and feed on polychaetes and crustacean larvae. They then retreat inland when salt water invades at the beginning of the low-water season.

Before they reach one year of age, piramutaba juveniles begin to inhabit estuarine streams and coastal lagoons, where they feed heavily on crustaceans and insects. Line-and-hook subsistence fishermen exploit these intermediate size classes. In areas near the ocean, such as Vigia, these fisheries take place mostly between January and May, when the Baía de Marajó is freshwater. At Gurupá, below the mouth of the Rio Xingu, fisheries for young piramutaba take place mostly between August and December, or during the low-water period of the Rio Amazonas. These two fishing patterns for piramutaba of intermediate size agree with the hypothesis that there is an inland migration of young fish when salt water invades during the low water period of the Rio Tocantins and Rio Amazonas. The fish move in the opposite direction when the Rio Amazonas and Rio Tocantins floods return and the salt water is pushed back out to sea.

Within the region of the southern part of the estuary outlined above, there is also a shrimp fishery based on *Macrobrachium amazonica*. This is the largest freshwater shrimp species in the Amazon Basin. Shrimp fishermen report that this crustacean migrates in a pattern very similar to that of young piramutaba. Because young piramutaba feed heavily on shrimp, there exists the possibility that predator follows prey. We believe, however, that both the catfish and the shrimp cannot tolerate salt water, and therefore the predator is not following prey as much as retreating from a potentially dangerous environment.

DOURADA MIGRATIONS IN THE AMAZON

Statistical data from fisheries and experimental fishing indicate that the migratory patterns of dourada are more complicated than those of piramutaba, and this is especially true of the Amazon estuary. Unlike piramutaba—and, in fact, most large catfish—dourada live in mid-depth to nearly surface waters. According to estuarine fishermen, dourada are able to move farther oceanward than are piramutaba. This makes sense ecologically, because the upper layers in the broad mixing zone where the Amazon River and Rio Tocantins meet the ocean are freshwater. The lower layers are assumed to be a salt wedge. Piramutaba, a bottom species, would not be able to survive as far seaward as the dourada.

As discussed above, industrial trawls employed to catch piramutaba in the estuary are used on the bottom. Dourada are thus only minimally vulnerable to this type of gear. Industrial operations in the estuary did not develop midwater or surface trawls to catch dourada because it was believed that these fish were either too low in biomass or too sparsely distributed to be captured in sufficient numbers with this gear. Most of our data for estuarine dourada are from small-scale fishing operations using gill nets.

Although dourada are midwater to surface fishes, they are still difficult to see in the muddy water of the estuary and inland rivers. As with piramutaba, fishermen depend on sightings of occasional dourada surfacing to indicate that schools or large groups are nearby. In river channels, dourada are commonly seen attacking prey at the surface, but this is not always an indication that schools or large groups are nearby.

Fisheries Indicating the Presence of Dourada

Unlike piramutaba, dourada is most heavily exploited upriver of the estuary. It is an important commercial species as far as the upper Rio Madeira and in Peru and Colombia. Pucallpa, Peru, 4,500 km upstream, is the farthest point from the estuary where there are market data for the dourada. It is the most important food fish species captured in the Rio Amazonas near Leticia, Colombia, and in the Rio Caquetá, Colombia (Salinas 1994; Muñoz Sosa 1993). Export markets for dourada first opened in the 1970s. In the case of Brazil, the new road network connecting the Amazon to the south made it possible to truck frozen fish to São Paulo and other states. An improved runway at Leticia allowed air transport to Bogotá. At present, dourada is exploited by the fishing fleets of every major town and city along the Amazon River and in the Rio Madeira, Rio Purus, Rio Juruá, and Rio Caquetá.

Geographical Distribution of Dourada Size Classes

The geographical distribution of dourada size classes was determined by analyzing commercial catches and through experimental fishing for young juveniles. Length measurements were obtained of 22,000 dourada from various areas of the Amazon River (estuary, Santarém, near Manaus, Tefé, and Leticia), the middle and upper Rio Madeira, the Rio Purus, and the Rio Juruá (figures 5.8 and 5.9) Most of the fish measured were captured in commercial operations with drifting deepwater gill nets. A large percentage of the dourada catch examined from the upper Rio Madeira was taken with gaffs. An additional 1000 measurements were gleaned from studies made by Salinas (1994) and Muñoz Sosa (1993) in the Rio Amazonas and Rio Caquetá respectively.

As with piramutaba, gill nets are highly selective in the dourada size classes they capture. Over 95 percent of the commercial catch consists of fish over 50 cm in length. In order to detect the presence of small size classes in areas and habitats not exploited by commercial operations, experimental fishing with gill nets was employed in the estuary and at various points along the Amazon River. Surveys carried out over many years have shown that dourada juve-

FIGURE 5.8
*Frequency Distribution of Dourada Size Classes Captured in the
Estuary, Lower Amazon, and Rio Madeira*

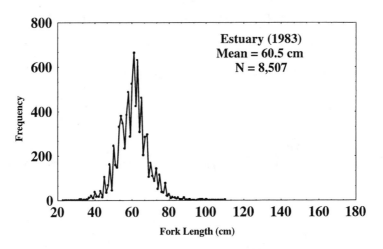

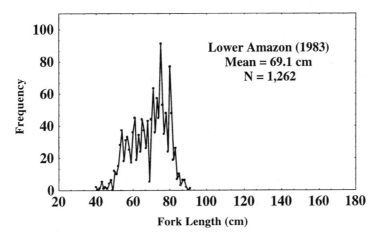

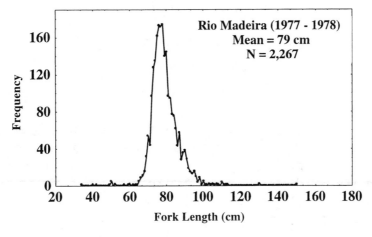

FIGURE 5.9

Frequency Distribution of Dourada Size Classes from the Central and Upper Amazon Region

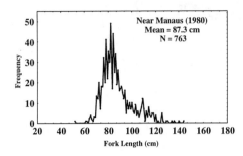

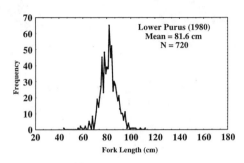

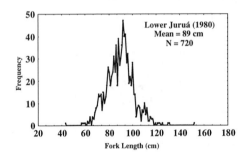

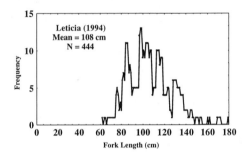

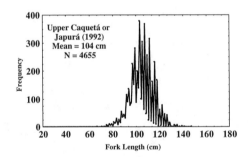

niles are not present on floodplains and preadults and adults only rarely enter these habitats.

Juvenile and preadult dourada are common in the estuary, but adults are rare or absent. The central Amazon appears to have mostly large preadult dourada. In the upper Amazon, adults are the most abundant size classes exploited. The modal size captured in the estuary by commercial operations is 70 cm; in the central Amazon near Manaus and upper Rio Madeira it is 80–90 cm; in the upper Amazon it is 90–110 cm.

Migratory Patterns of Preadult Dourada

Fishermen's reports, confirmed by market data from Belém and Santarém, clearly show that large numbers of dourada move upstream in the lower Rio Amazonas between August and October (figure 5.10). Dourada catches at Leticia, Colombia, are relatively high during the entire year (Salinas 1994). It is probable that these catches are made up of a mixture of resident fish, which arrived the previous year or earlier, and new recruits.

Were it not for the rapids of the upper Rio Madeira, we would probably not know that dourada also migrate at the beginning of the floods, as fishermen in other regions do not report these movements. Large fish are easily seen at Teotônio when they make their way through the turbulent waters (figures 5.11 and 5.12). There have been gaff fisheries for upstream-moving dourada at the Cachoeira do Teotônio since at least the early 1970s. These fisheries take place between December and February, when the river is rising rapidly. In some years, smaller groups of dourada also arrive at the Teotônio rapids during the low-water period (usually August and September), and this appears to be correlated with river levels lower than normal. The distance from the estuary to the Teotônio rapids is about 3,100 km. Dourada schools originating in the estuary would have to travel about 15–19 km/day in order to reach the Teotônio rapids in four to five months. This would be one of the fastest upstream fish migrations known for South America over such an extended period. Fish traveling this fast would not have time to feed. In the next chapter, we show that dourada feed heavily in the Central Amazon. Furthermore, fish arriving at the Teotônio rapids are on average considerably larger than the size classes captured in the lower Rio Amazonas and estuary (figure 5.13). This is not due to fish size selectivity in relation to gear. The gaffs used at the Teotônio rapids are effective for all size classes that pass the cataracts.

We hypothesize that migratory schools leaving the estuary disperse in river channels after reaching the Central Amazon in order to spend one to two years feeding (figure 5.14). This feeding area includes the huge lowland area west of and including the Rio Madeira to the pre-Andean plains. In the next chapter, we present data showing that dourada are major predators in the Central Amazon during the low- and rising-water periods. At the beginning of the annual floods, dourada that have been resident in the Central Amazon for at least a year school and move upstream. This may be considered a second migratory phase. The absence of developed gonads in dourada passing the Teotônio rapids of the Rio Madeira suggests that the purpose of these second-phase migrations is not immediate reproduction; instead, reproduction appears to be delayed for at

FIGURE 5.10
Monthly Catches of Dourada Along the Amazon River Based on Purchases by Refrigeration Plants

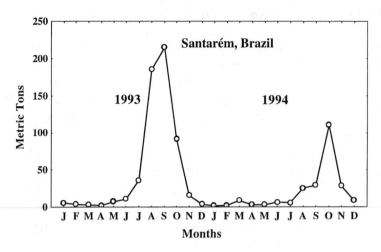

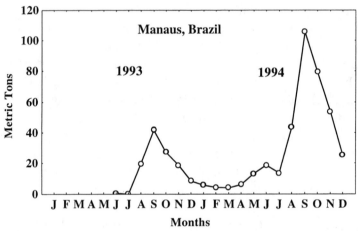

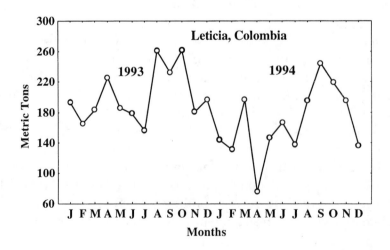

FIGURE 5.11

*Capturing Migratory Schools of Dourada During the Low-Water Season at the
Cachoeira do Teotônio of the Upper Rio Madeira*

FIGURE 5.12

Dourada Catch Taken in Turbulent Waters of the Upper Rio Madeira

FIGURE 5.13
A Dourada of Nearly Adult Size from the Upper Rio Madeira

Fish of this size probably spawn for the first time the year after reaching the head-water regions.

least a year. We assume that this same two-phase migratory pattern also takes place in the Amazon River but is not detected until mature fish reach the far western region near the Brazilian-Colombian-Peruvian border.

Reproduction

Large numbers of nearly or fully sexually mature dourada are only known for the Amazon River area near Leticia, and the Rio Caquetá in Colombia (Salinas 1994; Muñoz Sosa 1993; Barthem, personal observations). As mentioned above, fish in these areas also fall into larger size classes than those captured farther downstream. The mean size of sexually mature female dourada captured in the Leticia area was 112 cm (figure 5.15 and 5.16). Only 4 of the 22,000 dourada we examined from the central and lower Amazon had developed ovaries (figure 5.16). All these fish were larger than 110 cm.

Dourada are captured in large quantities during every month of the year in the Leticia area (Salinas 1994). There are still not enough data to pinpoint the

FIGURE 5.14

Growth Curve and Sexual Maturity of Dourada

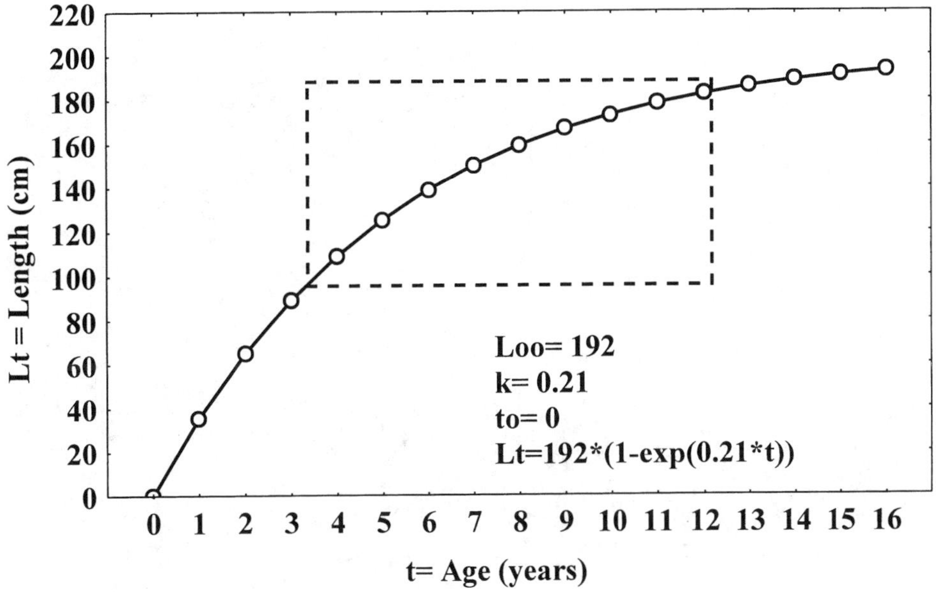

The box indicates the size range of sexually mature fish found thus far.
Growth data based on Salinas 1994 and Barthem 1990b.

exact months when dourada spawn in the upper Amazon, as Salinas (1994) and fishermen report the presence of mature fish during most of the year.

Downstream Migration of Dourada Larvae

To date the smallest dourada that have been captured were 6 cm. These fish were captured during experimental fishing in the Rio Solimões near Tefé during the low-water season (November) and at various locations in the estuary between April and June (Barthem specimens in Goeldi Museum). Zuanon (1990) also reports catching a 15 cm dourada during experimental fishing in the Rio Solimões near Manaus. The absence of sexually mature fish in the central and lower Amazon and estuary strongly suggests that dourada only spawn in the western Amazon (figure 5.17). The 6 cm dourada that have been captured in the estuary could be at a minimum fifteen days old. Fish born in the western Amazon could reach the estuary in thirteen to twenty days (see discussion above for piramutaba). We do not have enough specimens to determine whether dourada young might feed while descending the Amazon River.

FIGURE 5.15
*Ripe Dourada from the Rio Amazonas near Leticia, Colombia,
Being Prepared for Sale by Local Fishermen*

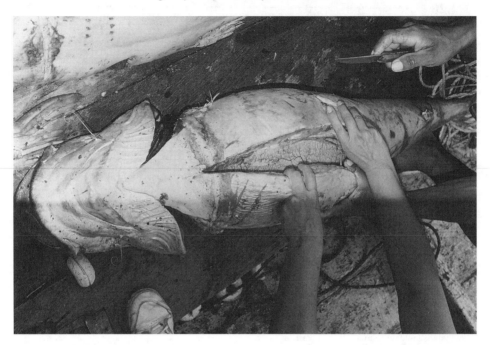

BABÃO MIGRATIONS

Babão (*Goslinia playtnema*) appear to be relatively rare compared to dourada
and piramutaba, although they, too, apparently make long-distance migrations that originate in the estuary. Barthem et al. (1991) report various size
classes of babão taken in the estuarine waters of the Baía de Marajó. The
species is of little commercial importance in the estuary. It is captured mostly
when migrating upstream at the same time as the dourada. Babão schools
arrive at the Teotônio rapids of the upper Rio Madeira as early as December,
but usually in January. They migrate through the rapids until at least mid-
March and as late as April in some years. At Teotônio, babão migrations at the
beginning of the floods seem to be about three to five weeks later than those
of dourada.

At least part of the babão population that migrates through the Teotônio
rapids consists of sexually mature fish. Muñoz Sosa (1993) found ripe babão in
the Rio Caquetá, where the species is exploited on a small scale commercially.
Interestingly, the size of the babão from the Rio Caquetá are smaller (70 cm)
than the average for populations that have been registered at the Teotônio

FIGURE 5.16
Adult Dourada Captured in the Upper Rio Madeira

Adult dourada are occasionally captured in the upper Rio Madeira, but there is no evidence of spawning in any area of the central Amazon.

FIGURE 5.17
Hypothesized Spawning (ellipse) and Nursery (box) Area of Dourada

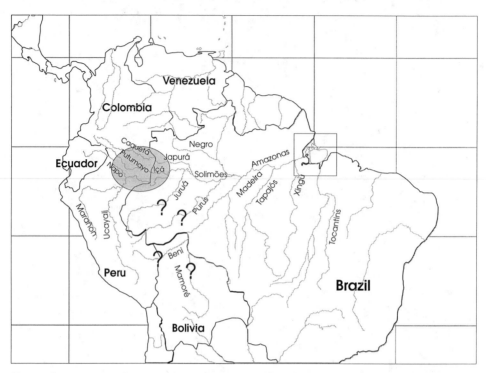

Dourada appear to have a larger spawning region than piramutaba, though large numbers of sexually mature fish have yet to be captured in the southwestern tributaries of the Amazon River.

than the average for populations that have been registered at the Teotônio cataracts of the upper Rio Madeira.

OTHER LARGE MIGRATORY CATFISH IN THE AMAZON

Other than the species discussed above, fishermen exploit at least nine other large catfish of the family Pimelodidae in the Amazon (see chap. 2). Most of these also appear to be migratory, but too few data are available to identify their seasonal movements. Of the nine species, only the piraíba (*Brachyplatystoma filamentosum*) is found in the estuary with dourada, piramutaba, and babão. Upstream migrations from the estuary, however, have not been reported or detected for this fish.

The large pimelodid catfishes are most easily seen at the Cachoeira de Teotônio between July and October, although they are heavily exploited over a wide part of the Amazon Basin as well. The caparari (*Pseudoplatystoma tigrinum*) and surubim (*Pseudoplatystoma fasciatum*) are the most important commercial species. They, too, are heavily exploited in floodplain waters. These predators appear to follow prey to river channels during low-water migrations.

The jaú (*Paulicea lutkeni*) is the most widely distributed large catfish in the Amazon Basin, although more than one species might be involved. The jaú is well known in South America for its habit of attacking migratory characins when these prey attempt to negotiate rapids. Because jaú appear seasonally at rapids, we assume that they make migrations to these habitats. This large, blubbery catfish has apparently evolved to live in rough waters without being battered to death. At the Teotônio rapids it can be seen feeding on characins and other fish that are attempting to move upstream.

6

Catfish as Predators

To understand the nature of predation in river channels and how the migration of dourada and piramutaba is linked to it, we examined the stomach contents of the five most important catfish species exploited in commercial fisheries. Of the 12,000 specimens studied, less than 8 percent contained prey. The low percentage of specimens with food in their stomachs does not mean that relatively few prey are available but rather that predators cannot maintain full or even half-full stomachs most of time. This is probably due to a high digestive rate, the short period of residence of food in the stomach, and regurgitation at the time of capture. Furthermore, a considerable amount of energy may be needed to capture prey, thus it may not be possible to maintain a full stomach between captures. On the other hand, when prey is ingested, it is highly nutritious, and this compensates for the amount of energy and time expended in catching it.

For the purposes of this study, we based predator-prey analyses on the estuary and inland river channels. Although catches examined from inland waters represented eight different sites in the central Amazon, all were from muddy river channels, and there were no significant differences in the main prey groups eaten. Little commercial fishing takes place during the high-water period because of the swollen river and huge amount of debris, such as logs and parts of floating meadows, being carried downstream. We suspect that feeding is greatly reduced for dourada, piramutaba, and piraíba during the high-water period because most prey move to the floodplains. The other predatory catfish, however, follow their prey to floodplain waters (Goulding 1980). It is possible that large catfishes remaining in river channels during the high-water period switch to different prey, but even these would be difficult to find in such an expanded environment.

Before discussing the nature and statistics of catfish predation, we provide an overview of the types of predators found in Amazonian rivers.

PREDATOR DIVERSITY IN RIVER CHANNELS AND THE ESTUARY

With perhaps the exception of the Orinoco, which has a very similar river-channel catfish fauna (Mago-Leccia 1970; Machado-Allison 1987; Novoa 1982), the Amazon Basin has more large predatory species (more than 50 cm in length) than any other freshwater system in the world. The main groups of Amazon fishes are characins, catfishes, gymnotoid electric fishes, and cichlids. Of these, only catfishes are important river-channel predators in the large muddy rivers.

South America has several species of large predatory characins that are found in river channels. None of these predators, however, has been able to disperse into the central part of the Amazon Basin. The most famous are dourados of the genus *Salminus*. Dourado, a characin, should not be confused with dourada, one of the main predatory catfish discussed in this work. Dourados, popular sport and food fish in southern Brazilian rivers, are known to make long upstream migrations in the Parará-Paraguay system (Godoy 1959, 1967, 1975; Bayley 1973). The genus *Salminus* is found in the Amazon Basin, but it is confined to headwater regions or areas associated with the Brazilian Shield.

Traíras of the genus *Hoplias* are a diverse group of characin fish of the family Erythrinidae. They are very widespread in both South and Central America. The largest species reach over 1 m in length and 20 kg in weight. All the large species, however, are restricted to the headwater regions of the Amazon or to rivers outside this basin.

The main predatory characins (more than 20 cm in length) found in Amazon river channels belong to the families Cynodontidae (dogtooth characins) and Ctenoluciidae (pike characins). Ctenoluciids are not commonly found in the open waters of channel habitats of muddy rivers but rather on their floodplains. They can be abundant in the river channels of some tributaries, however, and in headwater regions they can reach over 60 cm in length (Vari 1995). Dogtooth fishes of the genera *Raphiodon* and *Hydrolycus* are often abundant in the beach waters of river channels, but they are usually under 50 cm in length, whereas headwater forms of *Hydrolycus*, like some of the pike characins, are often more than 60 cm long.

The only large predator of the gymnotoids is the electric eel (*Electrophorus electricus*). This fish can reach nearly 3 m in length and weigh at least 15 kg. The snakelike bodies of electric eels make them poor swimmers in river-channel waters, however, and so they are confined mostly to floodplains or pools in streams.

The giant pirarucu (*Arapaima gigas*), reaching nearly 3 m in length and weighing over 150 kg, occasionally enters river channels to prey on migratory schools; for example, in the huge mouth area of the lower Rio Negro, it attacks migratory jaraqui characins of the genus *Semaprochilodus* (Ribeiro 1983). In the middle Rio Amazonas area near Santarém, we have also seen pirarucu in river channels. For the most part, however, this large predator lives in floodplain waters.

Of the families related to marine fishes, the bullshark, sawfish, and at least four or five species of stingrays are large predators in Amazon river channels. The bullshark and sawfish are not abundant enough to be important food fish, and for the most part they appear to be wanderers from the Atlantic. There are two families of stingrays in Amazon river channels, and some of the species reach over 1 m in length and 15 kg in weight (Rosa 1985). Both fishermen and our own experimental fishing suggest that stingrays are abundant enough to be exploited on a commercial basis. Stingrays are not commonly eaten in the Amazon, however, and there is only a very small market for them. It is thus difficult to judge how large their biomass might be.

The most diverse group of large predators in river channels is catfishes of the family Pimelodidae, of which there are at least twelve species. The pimelodids are only found in South and Central America, and all the large species are confined to South America. Furthermore, all but one of the large pimelodid catfishes are highly piscivorous as adults. Even the pirarara catfish (*Phractocephalus hemiliopterus*), which feeds mostly on fruits and crabs during the high-water season, will also eat fish during the low-water period. Only five of the twelve large predatory catfishes are commonly found on floodplains as well, while only one of the species that lives on floodplains is commonly found in the estuary. The estuary only has four species of large pimelodid catfishes.

In addition to fish, the boto and tucuxi dolphins and several species of otters are large predators in Amazon river channels. Otters rarely enter the larger rivers, except in tributaries or headwaters. The boto and tucuxi are widely distributed in the Amazon and are found both in river-channel and floodplain habitats and in the estuary. Caimans, which are crocodilians, can occasionally be seen in river channels, but for the most part they live near shore or in floodplain waters.

Catfish and dolphins are the principal predators in the channels of the muddy rivers of the lowland parts of the Amazon. Other than being large, their main shared characteristic is that they are both highly adapted to live in waters where visibility is no more than a few centimeters at best. The dolphins use sonar to navigate and locate their prey, while catfish have a highly developed organ called the Weberian apparatus that links the inner ear and swimbladder, and probably the lateral-line system as well. Roberts (1972) has characterized fish with the Weberian apparatus as being sound specialists. In the Amazon, characins and electric fishes also possess the Weberian apparatus. Most of the large catfish also have huge barbels—whiskers in popular terms—that they use to feel their way both forward and laterally. The dourada is an exception, except for individuals less than about 15 cm long. Catfish from many different families are known to be richly endowed with olfactory cells on their barbels and bodies.

Predatory catfish probably use all the above-mentioned senses to find their way and prey in muddy water. The visually oriented predators, such as dourado (*Salminus*), piranhas, peacock bass (*Cichla*), and traíra (*Hoplias*), probably cannot compete with the diverse predatory catfish assemblage, especially dourada and piramutaba, found in the channels of Amazonian muddy rivers

PREY DIVERSITY IN RIVER CHANNELS AND THE ESTUARY

All fish of any given habitat may be considered potential prey if a predator of sufficient size or with sharp enough teeth is present. After reaching about 50 cm length, the catfish have no significant predators. The boto dolphin is known to attack large catfish, but these are mostly doradids. In general, the boto prefers smaller prey, most of which are the same size as those that large catfish attack (Silva 1983). Fishermen report, however, that botos commonly attack catfish entangled in gill nets. They also report shark and sawfish attacks on large catfish, but these fish are too rare in the Amazon to be considered important predators. Other than large predatory catfish, stingrays appear to be the only abundant group that largely escapes predation. These fish have venom glands and stings on their tails. In addition, their disk-shaped bodies prevent predators from swallowing them easily, although small individuals are occasionally devoured.

The fish diversity in the Amazon River channel has not yet been reported in detail. Barletta (1995) sampled populations in 10–30 m deep waters in the Rio Solimões-Amazonas. At those depths, he captured approximately 60 species. In nearby floodplains, Bayley (1983) reported 325 species. Of the 450 fish species captured in a survey of the Rio Negro, about 250 were found in beach habitats of the river channel (Goulding, Carvalho, and Ferreira 1988). Ibarra and Stewart (1989) captured 208 species from beach waters of the Rio Napo in Ecuador. It thus seems probable that an intensive survey of the Amazon River channel, including beach waters, would reveal at least 250 species in any given 100-km stretch upriver of the estuary.

For the purposes of this study, fish prey were identified to the generic level (table 6.1 and figures 6.1, 6.2, 6.3, and 6.4).). A total of forty-seven genera, with perhaps sixty species, were found in the stomach contents of the eight predatory catfish species captured in river channels. The prey list includes most of the genera of medium-sized fish known to be in muddy river channels of the central Amazon. It can thus be concluded that, as a group, predatory catfishes prey on most of the medium-sized fish diversity that is present, though some species are more heavily attacked than others(see below).

TABLE 6.1

Prey Genera Identified from Large Predatory Catfishes of the Amazon

Group	Family	Dourada (*Brachyplatystoma flavicans*)	Piraiba (*Brachyplatystoma filamentosum*)	Piramutaba (*Brachyplatystoma vaillantii*)	Caparari (*Pseudoplatystoma tigrinum*)	Surubim (*Pseudoplatystoma fasciatum*)	Number of Individuals
Abramites	Anostomidae	0	0	0	0	4	4
Acestrorhynchus	Characidae	1	0	0	0	0	1
Achirus	Achiridae	0	1	0	0	0	1
Ageneiosus	Ageneiosidae	1	1	0	2	0	4
Anodus	Hemiodontidae	17	5	0	0	0	22
Astyanax	Characidae	1	0	0	0	0	1
Auchenipteridae	Auchenipteridae	4	0	0	0	0	4
Brycon	Characidae	0	1	0	1	3	5
Calophysus	Pimelodidae	1	8	0	0	0	9
Centromochlus	Auchenipteridae	1	0	8	0	0	9
Cetopsidae	Cetopsidae	12	19	1	0	0	32
Characidae	Characidae	35	8	1	3	2	49
Charax	Characidae	1	0	0	0	1	2
Cichlidae	Cichlidae	0	3	0	21	6	30
Colomesus	Tetraodontidae	0	5	0	0	0	5
Colossoma	Characidae	3	15	0	0	0	18

TABLE 6.1 (CONT'D.)

Group	Family	Dourada (*Brachyplatystoma flavicans*)	Piraíba (*Brachyplatystoma filamentosum*)	Piramutaba (*Brachyplatystoma vaillantii*)	Caparari (*Pseudoplatystoma tigrinum*)	Surubim (*Pseudoplatystoma fasciatum*)	Number of Individuals
Curimatidae	Curimatidae	56	24	0	50	47	177
Doras	Doradidae	18	42	30	7	3	100
Doradidae	Doradidae	0	1	0	0	01	2
Gymnotiformes	Gymnotiformes	12	29	9	1	0	51
Hemiodus	Hemiodontae	243	52	0	1	0	296
Hemisorubim	Pimelodidae	1	0	0	0	0	1
Hoplias	Erythrinidae	0	0	0	5	2	7
Hydrolycus	Cynodontidae	1	0	0	0	0	1
Hypophthalmus	Hyphthalmidae	14	14	0	2	0	30
Leporinus	Anostomidae	2	1	0	1	1	5
Loricariidae	Loricariidae	3	4	0	1	0	8
Metynnis	Characidae	2	0	0	0	0	2
Myleus	Characidae	0	1	0	2	0	3
Mylossoma	Characidae	24	13	0	5	1	43
Osteoglossum	Osteoglossidae	0	0	0	1	0	1
Oxydoras	Doradidae	0	1	0	0	0	1
Pachypops	Sciaenidae	0	1	0	0	0	1
Pareiodon	Trichomycteridae	1	1	0	0	0	2
Pellona	Clupeidae	9	7	0	0	0	16
Pimelodella	Pimelodidae	0	3	0	0	0	3
Pimelodidae	Pimelodidae	12	64	0	2	0	78
Pimelodus	Pimelodidae	20	48	17	7	3	95
Pinirampus	Pimelodidae	1	0	0	0	0	1
Plagioscion	Sciaenidae	1	2	0	3	0	6
Pristigaster	Clupeidae	2	0	0	0	0	2
Prochilodus	Prochilodontidae	2	3	0	4	2	11
Pseudoplatystoma	Pimelodidae	0	9	0	0	0	9
Pygocentrus	Characidae	1	0	0	5	2	8
Raphiodon	Cynodontidae	2	1	0	4	3	10
Rhytiodus	Anostomidae	4	3	0	1	0	8
Roeboides	Characidae	1	0	0	0	0	1
Schizodon	Anostomidae	3	2	0	3	0	8
Semaprochilodus	Prochilodontidae	9	117	84	4	2	216
Serrasalmus	Characidae	1	0	0	0	0	1
Sorubim	Pimelodidae	2	1	0	0	0	3
Triportheus	Characidae	58	28	6	19	11	122
Trichomycteridae	Trichomycteridae	0	4	0	0	0	4
Stingray	Potamotrygonidae	0	2	0	0	0	2
Total		582	544	156	155	94	1,531

FIGURE 6.1
Catfish Prey of the Characin Order (Characiformes)

A. *Semaprochilodus*; B. *Anodus*; C. *Rhytiodus*; D. *Hemiodus*; E. *Leporinus*; F. *Schizodon*;
G. *Psectrogaster*; H. *Potarmorhina*.

FIGURE 6.2
Catfish Prey of the Characin Order (Characiformes)

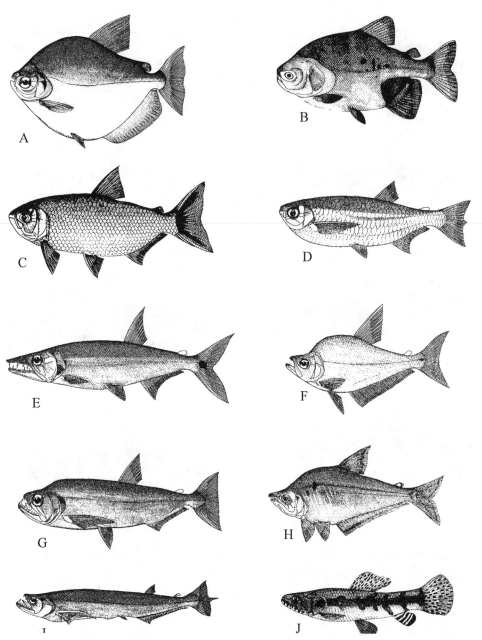

A. *Mylossoma*; B. *Colossoma*; C. *Brycon*; D. *Triportheus*; E. *Acestrorhynchus*; F. *Charax*;
G. *Hydrolycus*; H. *Roeboides*; I. *Raphiodon*; J. *Hoplias*.

FIGURE 6.3
Catfish Prey of the Catfish Order (Siluriformes)

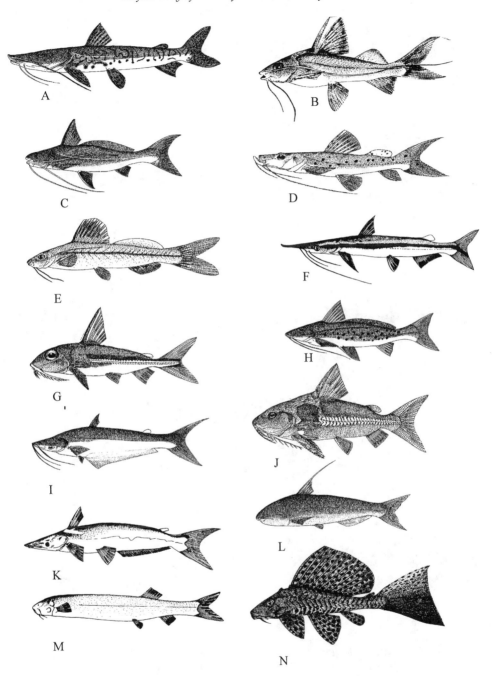

A. *Pseudoplatystoma*; B. *Pimelodus*; C. *Pinirampus*; D. *Hemisorubim*; E. *Pimelodella*;
F. *Sorubim*; G. *Hassar*; H. *Calophysus*; I. *Hypophthalmus*; J. *Doras*; K. *Ageneiosus*;
L. Cetopsidae; M. *Pareiodon*; N. *Pterygoplichthys*.

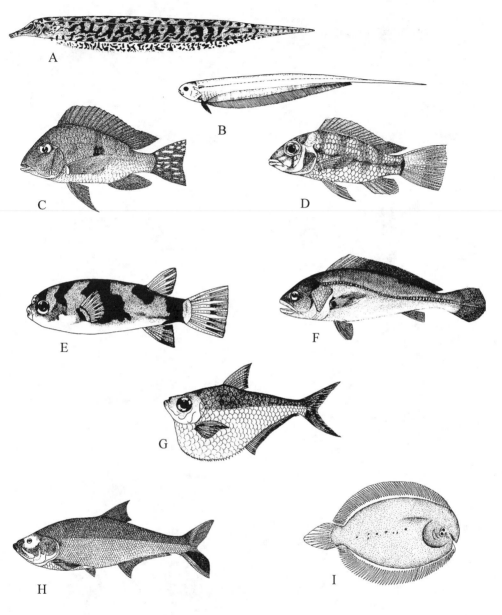

A. *Rhamphichthys*; B. *Eigenmannia*; C. *Geophagus*; D. *Satanoperca*; E. *Colomesus*; F. *Plagioscion*; G. *Pristigaster*; H. *Pellona*; I. Achiridae.

The fish diversity of the Amazon estuary—but not including the island of Marajó—is considerably lower than that found upstream in river channels. Barthem (1985) recorded fifty species for the Baía do Marajó. Only fifteen of the forty-five fish families found in river channels have been recorded for the Amazon estuary. On the other hand, there are sixteen marine or brackish-water families found in the estuary that are not found upstream. Many of these, however, are only present during the low-water period of the Amazon River when there is an invasion of salt water. In the estuary, dourada and pira-mutaba prey on relatively few fish and crustacean species, their main foods. Only three fish species in three families were identified as freshwater catfish prey in the estuary. No more than two shrimp (*Macrobrachium*) species are eaten. In terms of prey availability, the Amazon estuary may be classified as an area of high production but low diversity. This is true of nearly all large estuaries (Day et al. 1989).

PREY SELECTIVITY

Prey can be classified in several ways to test for selectivity by predators. Below we consider abundance, size, morphology, habitat preference, and schooling behavior. Nutrient and energy content might also be important, but we do not have enough data on this for the majority of prey species.

Prey Abundance

In a system with extremely high fish diversity, such as the Amazon, a piscivore could feed almost randomly on a large number of species. It is difficult to establish the relative and absolute abundance of prey species in river channels. Fisheries data, however, can also be used to determine if a species is abundant but not eaten by large catfish. If a species is an important food fish, then we assume here that it is also abundant.

For the most part, the prey list for large catfish reads like an inventory of the Manaus market (see table 6.1). It can thus be concluded that the large catfishes select prey species that are abundant in the sense defined above. Of the approximately fifty taxa of prey identified from catfish stomach contents, at least thirty-five are also food fishes in the Central Amazon. Nearly all the species captured in river channels for commercial fisheries are also preyed on by large catfishes. There are some exceptions. First, large predators do not prey on each other, because of size. Smaller caparari (*Pseudoplatystoma tigrinum*) and surubim (*Pseudoplatystoma fasciatum*), however, are preyed on by the other large catfish. Adult tambaqui (*Colossoma macropomum*) and pirapitinga (*Piaractus brachypomus*), both longer than 40 cm when adult, are important food fishes captured in river channels, but they are too large to be swallowed by catfish. The young of these species are confined to floodplains and so for the most part escape the river-channel predators. Some of the catfish feed on them in floodplains, but that is beyond the purview of this discussion.

Prey Size

Most of the fish species in the Amazon are small, or less than about 10 cm in length when adult (Weitzman and Vari 1988; Goulding, Carvalho, and Ferreira 1988). More than 95 percent of the prey eaten by the river-channel catfishes is larger than 10 cm. Therefore preadult and adult large catfishes select large prey relative to the average size of all species present. Of the 238 fish species captured in beach waters of the Rio Negro, only 36 percent were larger than an average of 10 cm in length. If the Amazon River channel has a similar distribution of fish sizes, then approximately 87 species of prey could theoretically be exploited by large catfish, although the majority of these would be rare. This suggests that large catfishes prey on most of the diversity present within the size classes they eat, although they are more likely to select some species because they are more abundant, more nutritious, or easier to catch.

It should be kept in mind that most of the small-fish diversity—and probably biomass as well, although this has not been shown—in muddy river channels is probably found in beach habitats during the low-water period or along shore zones that have floating plants. Although the large catfishes live in the river channel, not all of them move into shallow beach waters (less than 2 meters in depth) to feed. Only the surubim and caparari, species that also live on the floodplain, are commonly captured in beach waters. Araujo-Lima (1990) has shown that communities of small fish, such as anchovies (Engraulidae), also reside in the surface waters of the Amazon River channel beyond beach limits. Sampling habitats from 10 to 30 m deep, Barletta (1995) found the greatest diversity and biomass at depths of less than 10 meters, noting that postlarvae and juveniles of various catfishes, dogtooth characins, and croakers used benthic habitats for what he believed to be protection, feeding, and dispersal. These benthic habitats, however, are much lower in fish biomass than floodplain habitats, such as floating meadows (see Bayley 1983 for floodplain data). Relatively low biomass of small fish per area is probably the main factor explaining why there are no important fisheries in river channels based on predators that feed mostly on small prey. The floodplains have several species of predators that feed on small fish, the tucunarés (*Cichla* spp., Cichlidae) being the most important in commercial fisheries

Predator-Prey Ratio

The length of prey eaten by the large catfishes varies between 1.2 and 59 cm. Within that range, regression analysis indicates a linear relationship between size of predator and prey when all prey groups are considered together (table 6.2 and figure 6.5). At the prey-species level, however, there is no obvious relationship between size of predator and prey. This is probably because most river-channel prey are preadult or adult medium-sized fish. For example, the young, that is, smaller size classes, of the migratory characins are confined mostly to the floodplains, hence predatory catfishes have no opportunity to eat them in river channels

TABLE 6.2

Correlation Coefficients for Predator-Prey Ratios as Shown in Figure 6.5

Prey (cm) = a + b* Predator (cm)	Piraíba (*Brachyplatystoma filamentosum*)	Dourada (*Brachyplatystoma flavicans*)	Piramutaba (*Brachyplatystoma vaillantii*)	Caparari (*Pseudoplatystoma tigrinum*)	Surubim (*Pseudoplatystoma fasciatum*)
Sample Size (*N*)	494	766	136	163	96
Significance of Regression (*P*)	<0.001	<0.0001	<0.0001	<0.0001	<0.0001
a	4.043	4.403			
b	0.103	0.148	0.607	0.171	0.171
Pearson Correlation (*R*)	0.17	0.46	0.42	0.41	0.41

Morphology

Morphologically, the fish groups eaten by predatory catfishes are relatively uniform at the family or subfamily level. These prey can be classified as spindle-shaped (fusiform), compressed, depressed, serpentine, or flattened. In order to test for selectivity, we divided prey by family or subfamily into those morphological groups. Flattened fishes, which include stingrays and soles, are the only morphological group of the five that is of relatively little importance. As mentioned earlier, stingrays are more abundant than fisheries data indi-

FIGURE 6.5
Predator-Prey Ratios

Dourada
Brachyplatystoma flavicans

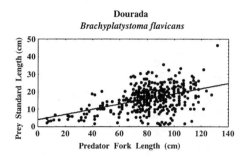

Piramutaba
Brachyplatystoma vaillantii

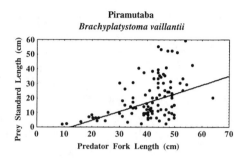

Piraíba
Brachyplatystoma filamentosum

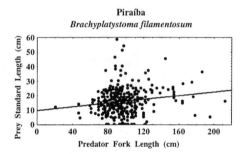

Surubim
Pseudoplatystoma flavicans

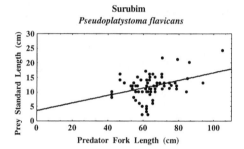

Caparari
Pseudoplatystoma tigrinum

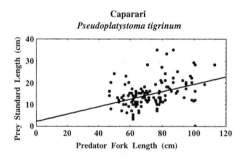

cate. As noted, catfish cannot feed on these flattened species because of their venom and because they cannot easily swallow individuals greater than about 25 cm. The other flattened species, Amazonian soles, do not appear to be abundant enough to be major prey. In addition, they tend to remain hidden in the sand or mud and so may be difficult to find or capture.

The large catfish have a slight preference for spindle-shaped fish

(Prochilodontidae, Curimatidae, Hemiodontidae, and Characidae). Fish belonging to these families represented about 40 percent of the total prey volume found in all stomach contents. Spindle-shaped fish are especially important to dourada and piraíba, representing 89 and 59 percent, respectively, of the total volume of prey consumed. The importance of these prey may be related more to their schooling behavior than their morphology (we discuss schooling in more detail in a later section).

Catfish account for most of the morphologically depressed species, and they are the second most important group eaten by predators. The sharp and pungent dorsal and pectoral fin spines of catfish do not seem to deter the large predators, at least in the size classes of prey that they eat. We have examined dourada and piraíba specimens with perforated and/or scarred stomachs caused most likely by catfish spines. This suggests that the predators can heal major stomach wounds.

The main serpentine-shaped prey are gymnotiform electric fishes. Amazonian electric fishes are not captured in commercial fisheries because there is so little meat on them. Recent surveys suggest that gymnotiforms are relatively abundant in the Amazon River channel (Barletta 1995; John Lundberg, pers. comm.). The fact that predatory catfish prey regularly on them also confirms their abundance in river channels. Because electric fishes are so thin, they are probably digested faster than other prey are, thus stomach content analyses might slightly—but not grossly, in our opinion—underestimate their importance in catfish diets.

The only compressed fish abundant in river channels are pacus (Serrasalminae), to which the piranhas are related. (Piranhas are not common in the river channels of muddy rivers, although they can occasionally be found in some numbers in quiet side channels.) The largest members of the pacu group are the tambaqui (*Colossoma macropomum*) and pirapitinga (*Piaractus brachypomus*). The juveniles of these species are restricted mostly to floodplains, but adults enter the river channels during the low-water season. As mentioned earlier, adult tambaqui and pirapitinga are too large to be eaten by the predatory catfish. The most common pacus in muddy water belong to the genus *Mylossoma*. These fish rarely exceed 25 cm in length and can be swallowed by the catfish. It is possible that body compression makes them more difficult to grab than the spindle-, depressed- and serpentine-shaped prey discussed above, but experimental laboratory evidence will be needed to test this assumption.

Water Depth Inhabited by Prey

The general perception of catfish is that they are bottom creatures. If this were strictly true, then it would be safe to assume that their prey must be bottom dwellers as well. Catfish, however, are much more flexible in terms of the water depths they inhabit than the stereotype suggests. The vertical distribution of the prey eaten by the predatory catfish of Amazonian river channels demonstrates this.

Too little information is available for us to pinpoint the exact depths that river-channel fishes prefer. Based on long personal observation and fishermen's reports, however, we feel we can safely divide the species into three main categories: bottom, surface, and combination. We will not attempt to assign exact depths to these categories. By *bottom*, we mean that the species lives mostly somewhere between mid-depth and the bottom; the surface is the corresponding upper layer. A few species, and especially some of the predators, are commonly found at both depths. If we had more information, many of these might be classified as mid-depth fishes.

As a group the predatory catfishes exploit the entire water column for their prey. All the predatory species also feed to some extent in the entire water column, though a few species manifest very strong depth preferences. The dourada, surubim, and caparari feed mostly on fishes living in the surface layer; piramutaba feed mostly on bottom fishes. Surubim and caparari appear to feed closer to the shore, especially in beach waters, than do the other species. Although more data are needed, the babão appears to feed mostly on the bottom. In terms of water depth and prey diversity, the piraíba is the most versatile of the large predators. It is often seen jumping out of the water and attacking fishes at the surface—its common name in Colombia is saltator, or jumper—but it is most commonly captured on the bottom with trotlines.

During the low-water period, surubim, caparari, and even, to a certain extent, dourada move into beach waters at night to feed on prey. The distinction between surface and bottom communities is less clear in shallow beach waters. Large schools of characins, for example, occupy the entire water column in beach waters, though they would not be considered bottom fishes midriver.

Schooling

The most important food fishes in the Amazon are migratory and form large schools on a seasonal basis (Goulding 1988). Schooling places huge numbers of fish together in a relatively small space. This makes them attractive to predators, including fishermen. Ecologists, however, generally agree that schooling is an antipredator adaptation (Lowe-McConnell 1987; Cushing and Harden-Jones 1968). Schooling theoretically makes it more difficult for a predator to focus on an individual prey, and this appears to be especially true in clear waters (Partridge 1982). We do not know to what extent schooling represents antipredator behavior in muddy water, such as the Amazon River, where catfish do not usually see their prey but rather locate them with a combination of senses involving the detection of water motion, touch, hearing, and olfaction. It is possible, however, that the confusion of sounds and smells made by a prey school could help confuse a predator relying on these means to locate an individual prey

The large catfishes heavily exploit migratory characins. These are basically the same species exploited in the commercial fisheries in the Amazon. Fishermen believe, and our data confirm, that the dourada and piraíba are highly tuned to characin migrations. During characin migrations, dourada and piraíba can be seen attacking schooling fish. Approximately 97 percent of the prey biomass eaten by dourada were migratory characins. As far as is known, the other predatory catfishes do not rely so heavily on migratory characins. Although we have observed the piramutaba feeding on upstream migrating schools of *Triportheus* (a characin), this does not seem to be a regular practice.

OVERLAP IN DIETS OF LARGE CATFISHES

The large predatory catfishes in Amazonian river channels have evolved to use nursery habitats that allow the young of each species to be separated from most, though never all, of the other species. It would seem that this geographical separation of predatory catfish juveniles developed as a way to reduce competition for food and habitat space, though other factors, such as oxygen levels, might have been the initial factors that led to present patterns (see chap. 7). Whatever the case, the geographical separation of large biomasses of young fish does theoretically reduce competition.

Dourada and piramutaba use the estuary as their main nursery habitats. But even there the young occupy different habitats. The piramutaba feed mostly on gobies and crustaceans found on the bottom, while young dourada feed heavily on surface fishes such as anchovies. The young of surubim and caparari are found mostly on the floodplains, but we have too few data to know whether they live in different habitats and what they eat. Surveys have shown that piraíba size classes under about 35 cm are not common on floodplains. Midsize piraíba ranging from 35 to 60 cm are common in floodplain waters and exploited commercially, but there is considerable discussion among taxonomists as to whether these are the same species that is found in river channels. In any case, larval, postlarval, and juvenile piraíba have been captured by us and others in river channels and in the estuary (Barthem, Ribeiro, and Petrere Jr. 1991; Barletta 1995). It should be noted that the estuary has no known large populations of juvenile piraíba on the scale of the massive quantities of dourada and piramutaba found in those waters. We believe that juvenile piraíba use river channels—including muddy, clearwater, and blackwater rivers—and parts of the estuary as nursery habitats.

The greatest overlap in diet occurs once the various species, at preadult or adult size, migrate from their respective nursery habitats, either in the estuary or on the floodplains, to the river channels. On a geographical basis, the main theater of competition for preadult and adults is in the channels of muddy rivers in the central and western Amazon. This is the region with the greatest fish (prey) production, because of the foodchains linked to floodplain forests, lakes, and floating meadows. Fish, like fishermen, migrate to this area seasonally to exploit prey.

None of the preadult or adult predatory catfish found in the river channels are highly specialized as to individual prey species. The seasonality of prey abundance is the main factor that prevents this. This seasonality is clearly shown by Manaus market data, which also reflects the migratory patterns of many of the characins (e.g., Petrere Jr. 1978b, 1985a). No prey group of major importance was found to be eaten exclusively by one predatory species; instead, the ten most important prey groups were all eaten by at least three, and usually four, catfish species. Dourada and piraíba prey more heavily on migratory characin groups than do the other large catfish.

When it is not possible to determine available food resources, the frequency of kinds of prey eaten by predators can give a general idea of the overlap in diets. We used Morisita's Simplified Index to calculate overlap (Krebs 1989). In this index, a value of 1.0 would mean complete overlap (table 6.3). Only the surubim (*Pseudoplatystoma fasciatum*) and caparari (*Pseudoplatystoma tigrinum*) showed extremely high overlap, or about 0.9. Both of these species feed mostly in beach waters when in river channels, thus they are largely separated from the other large predators. Piraíba (*Brachyplatystoma filamentosum*) and piramutaba (*Brachyplatystoma vaillantii*) also had considerable overlap (.68). This is largely due to the bottom prey species, especially doradid and pimelodid catfishes, that they share. Overall, the diet of the dourada (*Brachyplatystoma flavicans*) appears to have the least amount of overlap with that of the other predatory catfishes. This is probably because it feeds throughout the water column, though with a preference for mid- to surface waters. The dourada's greatest overlap is with piraíba, a species that also feeds in the entire water column. The piraíba, however, feeds more on bottom prey.

TABLE 6.3
Prey Overlap in Predatory Catfish Diets Based on Morisita's Simplified Index

Species	Caparari (*Pseudoplatystoma tigrinum*)	Dourada (*Brachyplatystoma flavicans*)	Piraíba (*Brachyplatystoma filamentosum*)	Piramutaba (*Brachyplatystoma vaillantii*)	Surubim (*Pseudoplatystoma fasciatum*)
Caparari	1	0.285	0.318	0.136	0.901
Dourada		1	0.446	0.083	0.255
Piraíba			1	0.679	0.214
Piramutaba				1	0.089
Surubim					1

Although the data show overlap in the predators' diets, the partitioning of different habitats in the river channel may be more subtle than stomach contents alone indicate. This can only be true, however, if prey of the same species occupy various depths within the river channel and predators divide themselves among these zones

FOODCHAINS AND LARGE CATFISHES IN RIVER CHANNELS

The foodchain ecology of Amazonian fishes has been studied from three perspectives: flooded forests, floating meadows, and plankton production in floodplain lakes (see, e.g., Goulding 1980; Bayley 1983; Araujo-Lima et al., 1986). It is now known that these are the three main sources of primary production that sustain Amazonian fishes. The relative value of each varies with river type and floodplain size.

The diets of the large predatory catfishes give a strong indication of the nature of the foodchains in the channels of Amazonian muddy rivers. To quantify the nature of the foodchains sustaining large catfishes, we divided their prey into seven categories based on the most important foods they eat. These categories are:

1. *Detritus/Algae*: Species feeding on these items are often called microphagous fish because of the minute nature of the foods they eat. Detritus often contains algae, bacteria, fungi, and tiny animals. The characin families Prochilodontidae, Curimatidae, and Hemiodontidae

account for most of the microphagous species. All these are migratory species.

2. *Fruit and invertebrates*: Most prey species that feed heavily on fruits and seeds, especially the pacus, also consume considerable quantities of insects as well, thus the two food sources are grouped together.

3. *Aquatic invertebrates.*

4. *Terrestrial invertebrates.*

5. *Fish.*

6. *Plankton*: Most of the prey species in this group are zooplanktivorous.

7. *Highly mixed.*

Our data strongly suggest that the foodchain tied to plankton, detritus, and other small items washed into the river channel is of much less importance to the large catfishes than is the huge biomass of prey fish that migrates from the floodplains to the river channels on a seasonal basis. Primary production in the channels of muddy rivers is minimal because of the lack of light. These muddy rivers, however, do receive huge quantities of organic material, including detritus, phytoplankton, zooplankton, and other microinvertebrates and parts of floating meadows that are washed out of floodplains or, to a lesser extent, discharged by clearwater and blackwater tributaries. Lundberg et al. (1987) has shown that a similar situation occurs in the Orinoco and that major foodwebs involving floodplain and terrestrial food sources have evolved in the river channel. The study emphasizes the importance of gymnotiform electric fishes in tapping planktonic crustaceans and insect larvae. Field investigations by the present authors indicate that a similar situation occurs in the Amazon River, but this has not yet been studied in detail.

In order to calculate the relative biomass importance of different types of prey in catfish diets, we extrapolated prey weights from lengths, based on length-weight regressions already in our databases at the Museu Goeldi (table 6.4). Of the thirty-five principal prey groups found in the catfish specimens examined, 75 percent of the biomass consisted of microphagous species. The dourada fed more on microphagous species than did the other predatory catfishes, with 87 percent of the biomass of their diet consisting mostly of detritus feeders or algae feeders. The ability of the dourada to exploit surface waters largely explains why it is able to prey on these species. The second most important foodchain level tapped by the catfishes consisted of prey species that feed heavily both on fruits and seeds and on invertebrates that fall into the water. These are mostly the pacu (*Mylossoma*) fishes. Nearly as important were piscivores. Prey feeding mostly on terrestrial invertebrates, plankton, or large numbers of items were of only minimal importance to the catfishes.

TABLE 6.4

Percentages of Prey Wet Weights in the Main Trophic Categories
for Each of the Predatory Catfishes Studied

Trophic Category of Prey	Babão (*Goslinia platynema*)	Caparari (*Pseudoplatystoma tigrinum*)	Dourada (*Brachyplatystoma flavicans*)	Piraíba (*Brachyplatystoma filamentosum*)	Piramutaba (*Brachyplatystoma vaillantii*)	Pirarara (*Phractocephalus hemiliopterus*)	Surubim (*Pseudoplatystoma fasciatum*)	Mean
Microphagous	0	35	87	62	0	51	73	44
Aquatic Invertebrates	56	15	1	4	75	48	4	29
Piscivorous	44	5	3	13	10	0	0	11
Fruits and Invertebrates	0	17	3	12	13	0	4	7
Omnivorous	0	15	1	4	1	1	19	6
Planktivorous	0	4	4	4	0	0	0	2
Terrestrial Invertebrates	0	8	0	0	0	0	0	1

Comparative Manaus data based on Petrere Jr. 1985a.

We are still uncertain of the extent to which piramutaba feed in the central and western Amazon. Unlike the fisheries for dourada, which take place for five to eight months of the year, those for piramutaba are concentrated in the few months that the species is migrating upstream. As mentioned earlier, we have seen piramutaba attacking upstream-migrating characins. Furthermore, specimens examined from piramutaba schools in the lower Rio Amazonas showed that the species feeds at least to some extent when migrating. Most of the prey are bottom or deepwater fishes of the families Doradidae (armored catfish), Pimelodidae (long-whiskered catfishes), and gymnotiform electric fishes. These prey primarily feed on aquatic invertebrates, though some species are also highly omnivorous. The piramutaba, more than any of the other large catfishes, may be tapping the part of the foodweb that is linked to the plant and animal material, including detritus, that is washed into the river channels from floodplains and tributaries. If piramutaba feed more heavily in the central and western Amazon than our data indicate, then the importance of the organic wash from floodplains to river channels is probably also more important.

FOODCHAINS AND CATFISHES IN THE ESTUARY

Young dourada (less than 70 cm) in the estuary feed heavily on four to six species of anchovies (Engraulidae), including both zooplanktivores and piscivores. The piscivorous anchovies feed on zooplanktivores of their own family. The dourada-anchovy link is connected to phytoplankton. The foodchain leading to the gobies, croakers, and crustaceans eaten by dourada is linked both to phytoplankton and organic material deposited by the Amazon River and the Rio Tocantins.

In the open waters of the estuary, piramutaba less than 5 cm feed heavily on shrimp larvae, polychaetes, and annelids. Both shrimp and polychates feed on organic matter found on or near the bottom. Piramutaba young do not remain long in open waters after arriving in the estuary but at about 5 cm length migrate to inundated shore areas, including those of islands, to inhabit streams, inlets, and outer parts of the tidal forests. Piramutaba only leave these habitats after reaching about 20 cm in length, or more than one year of age. In shore habitats they feed most heavily on shrimp.

Mud-dwelling gobies (perhaps three species) are the most important prey eaten by subadult and adult piramutaba (more than 20 cm) in the estuary. Gobies feed mostly on organic detritus and invertebrates found in the bottom mud. No other large Amazonian catfish specializes on prey species to the extent that the piramutaba does on gobies.

INTERACTIONS OF DOLPHINS AND PREDATORY CATFISHES

Other than catfishes, and leaving fisheries aside, dolphins are the only other large predators commonly found in the open waters of the channels of Amazonian muddy rivers. The diets of Amazonian dolphins in river channels have not yet been studied in detail, although Silva (1983) analyzed boto (*Inia geoffrensis*) and tucuxi (*Sotalia fluviatilis*) diets in (mostly) floodplain waters by identifying fish otoliths recovered from stomach contents. On floodplains, dolphins were found to feed heavily on croakers. These fish are relatively unimportant to large catfishes, probably because croakers live mostly on floodplains

Most of the genera of prey fed on by dolphins are also prey of the large catfishes. Indeed, dolphins are often seen attacking migratory schools in river channels. They follow fish schools for several days and are frequently seen grabbing prey that tries to escape at the surface or by jumping out of the water. We have observed dolphins attacking nearly all the migratory characins captured in commercial fisheries. For fishermen, the presence of dolphins signals the proximity of migratory fish schools.

Dolphins can feed throughout the water column. Depending on the exact situation, they probably have considerable diet overlap with large catfishes. Silva's (1983) data indicate that on the floodplain the boto explores a wide range of depths and habitats, whereas the tucuxi tends to favor pelagic waters. It would be very interesting to know if this pattern is repeated in river channels.

PREDATORY CATFISH VERSUS COMMERCIAL FISHERIES

The extent to which fisheries and predatory catfish compete is complicated to assess because it is so difficult to gather data on the constantly changing biomasses of the many prey species present in the Amazon. As mentioned earlier, catfishes eat most of the same species that commercial fisheries exploit. Competition in an evolutionary sense, however, can only exist if the quantity of prey available is limited relative to the needs of predators, including fisheries. Because fisheries also heavily exploit the catfishes, thus removing a large part of the predatory biomass, this would also seem to decrease the potential for competition.

In the estuary, piramutaba and dourada are the most important commercial species, and there is very little overlap in the fish species they eat (especially gobies and anchovies) and those captured in the commercial fisheries. Little is yet known about shrimp fisheries in the freshwater part of the estuary, and it is possible that piramutaba and dourada compete with commercial operations for these crustaceans in this area. The industrial shrimp fisheries near the Amazon estuary are located in salt water to the northeast and east of the island of Marajó, habitats that the large freshwater catfishes do not enter.

To determine to what extent fisheries and predatory catfishes might compete, we calculated the quantity of prey dourada would eat in a one-year period. We considered only this species because it is the most important large catfish exploited in river channels and we have the most information on it. Based on landings in Belém, Santarém, Parintins, Manaus, Leticia, and Iquitos during the 1992–1994 period, approximately 4,140 tons of dourada were captured annually in the Amazon. Using length-weight regression, we calculated the theoretical weight of individual prey that the dourada would consume during a one-year period. We arrived at the amount of prey eaten in a one-year period based on the assumption that a predator ingests an average of 1 percent of its body weight per day. The composition of prey was based on stomach content analyses and divided into families. We also assumed that the total dourada biomass present in the Amazon River is at least four times greater than annual catches of this catfish, thus the quantity of prey theoretically eaten would be at least four times greater as well. The quantity of prey eaten by dourada was then compared to Manaus annual catches, based on Petrere Jr.'s (1985a) data. Manaus is not only the largest fish market of the central and western Amazon, but its fleet also exploits a huge region that includes most of the large tributaries

Assuming that the dourada biomass in Amazon river channels is at least 16,560 tons, this predatory catfish alone eats 57,928 tons of prey. This is more fish than the total consumed in Manaus annually (table 6.5). Most overlap in the prey eaten by dourada and captured by Manaus fisheries occurs with migratory characins of medium size. All the important prey species eaten by dourada are also among the twenty most common food fishes in Manaus. For six of the eight families in this group, dourada consumes more prey tonnage than is captured by Manaus fisheries. Bayley and Petrere Jr. (1989) estimated that annual commercial and subsistence fish catch in the Amazon was about 200,000 tons. If dourada alone consume at least 60,000 tons of prey annually, then the five main predatory catfishes together must take over 100,000 tons—at least half the amount consumed or exported by the human population in the Amazon.

TABLE 6.5

The Theoretical Percentages of Prey Eaten by Dourada in Comparison to the Average Annual Manaus Catch

Group	Manaus Average Annual Catch (in Tons)	Prey (in Tons) Consumed by Average Annual Dourada Catch in River Channels	Percentage of Total Prey Consumed by Dourada (Manaus Annual Average Catch + Prey Eaten by Average Annual Dourada Catch)	Prey (in Tons) Consumed by Theoretical Total Dourada Biomass (16,560 Tons) in River Channels	Percentage of Total Prey Eaten by Total Dourada Biomass in River Channels vs. Manaus Average Annual Catch
Cetopsidae	0	162	100	648	100
Doradidae	0	88	100	352	100
Engraulidae	0	2	100	8	100
Gymnotiformes	0	33	100	132	100
Hemiodontidae	4,982	4,898	50	19,592	80
Clupeidae	100	97	49	388	80
Hypophthalmidae	1,260	1,218	49	4,872	79
Pimelodidae	391	355	48	1,420	78
Prochilodontidae	15,273	6,902	31	27,608	64
Curimatidae	740	201	21	804	52
Serrasalminae: *Mylossoma*	1,623	194	11	776	32
Characidae (*Brycon, Triportheus*)	1,761	207	11	828	32
Anostomidae	1,234	121	9	484	28
Sciaenidae	278	4	1	16	5
Cichlidae	1,072	0	0	0	0

Serrasalminae: *Piaractus*	1,509	0	0	0	0
Serrasalminae: *Colossoma*	13,596	0	0	0	0
Osteoglossidae	452	0	0	0	0
Loricariidae	170	0	0	0	0
Arapaimidae	166	0	0	0	0
Total	**44,607**	**14,482**		**57,928**	

Note: Comparisons are based on an average annual dourada catch of 4,140 tons and a theoretical total dourada biomass of 16,560 tons (excluding estuary). High values indicate that dourada consume a much larger proportion of the prey group present than is captured by Manaus fishermen.

7

Conclusion

The evolutionary history of the South American fish fauna is extremely complex, and the Amazon Basin is probably the most difficult region to understand because of its size, geological diversity, and huge numbers of species whose geographical origins are unclear (Menezes 1970; Weitzman and Weitzman 1982). Little fossil evidence has yet been presented that might throw light on how ancient dourada or piramutaba might be geologically. Fossils of large catfishes from the upper Miocene, however, have been found in Colombia, and these include the genus *Brachyplatystoma*, to which dourada and piraíba belong (Lundberg, Machado-Allison, and Kay 1986; Lundberg, tel. con., 1996). At least one other migratory fish in the Amazon, the tambaqui (*Colossoma macropomum*, Characidae), has also been found in Miocene deposits as old as fifteen million years (Lunderg, Machado-Allison, and Kay 1986). Like tambaqui, dourada and piramutaba are also common in the Orinoco basin.

No evidence suggests what catfish migrations in the Amazon Basin might have been like before the rise of the Andes. No extant large catfishes are known west of the Andes. If fossils of either dourada or piramutaba were to be found west of the Andes, this would strongly suggest that these fishes once used a Pacific coast estuary as a nursery, more than fifteen million years ago. This would supposedly be the estuary of the Amazon River when and if it flowed to the Pacific before the rise of the Andes. Some evidence suggests that ten million years ago, after the rise of the Andes, a major Miocene seaway might have run north-south from the mouth of the Orinoco in Venezuela to the La Plata in Argentina and east to what is now the mouth of the Amazon (Webb 1995). Most of the lowland Amazon Basin would have been submerged in seawater. If this geological interpretation is correct, then dourada and piramutaba would have been confined at that time to rivers of the Brazilian and Guiana Shields and/or to the eastern Andean area, as what is now the Amazon River would have been part of a vast inland sea. Although dourada and piramutaba now use the Amazon River and its muddy Andean tributaries as the main route for upstream migrations, Miocene remnant patterns may occur in some Brazilian or Guiana Shield rivers. For example, schools of dourada are known to migrate upstream in the Rio Branco in Roraima, but we do not yet have any data showing whether spawning takes place in these headwaters. This region is part of the ancient Guiana Shield. That dourada still migrates to Guiana Shield headwaters may echo patterns that were prevalent before the muddy Andean tributaries came to dominate the ecology of the lowland rivers of the Amazon Basin. Hoorn, Guerrero, and Sarmiento (1995) have also presented evidence that the Amazon River might have been connected to the paleo-Orinoco sometime subsequent to the late Miocene. Perhaps dourada and piramutaba migrations first evolved in an Amazon River that flowed north and drained toward the Caribbean. This would explain why the Orinoco and Amazon have the same species of large predatory catfishes. It should also be kept in mind, however, that dispersal would have been possible along the east coast of South America between the Amazon and Orinoco estuaries because of the huge amount of freshwater discharged northward by the Amazon. Dourada and piramutaba are, in fact, found in French Guiana, Suriname, and Guyana. Finally, upper Rio Negro waters of the Amazon Basin are connected to Orinoco headwaters via the Casiquiare Canal, and this is another possible dispersal route.

The present geological backdrop reveals the following patterns: (1) the estuary, that is, the area of highest primary production, became the nursery for the large catfish; (2) the muddy rivers of the central Amazon, that is, the area where the largest biomass of inland-water fish is found, became the main feeding habitats for preadult and adult dourada, but to a lesser extent for piramutaba; (4) adult dourada became excluded from the estuary, whereas piramutaba return there after spawning; (5) the western Amazon became the main spawning area for dourada and piramutaba, and probably some other large migratory catfishes as well (figure 7.1).

FIGURE 7.1

A Generalized Model of Dourada (below) and Piramutaba (above) Migration in the Amazon

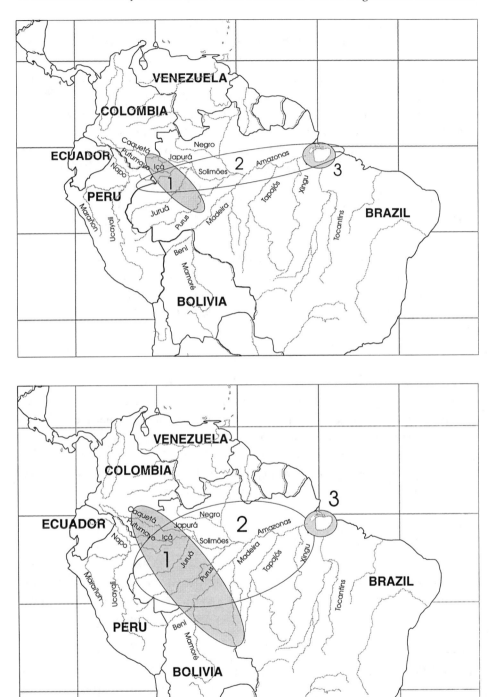

Note: 1 = hypothesized spawning region; 2 = feeding area of adults and preadults; 3 = nursery area.

The geographical separation of adult and juvenile populations is a common phenomenon among migratory fishes (Nikolsky 1963; Lowe-McConnell 1987; McDowall 1988). Young fish usually occupy the areas with the highest primary production. In the case of the Amazon, this can only be the floodplains or estuary: the amount of food available in river channels is too low to support the large populations of piramutaba and dourada found in the estuary.

Any hypothesis attempting to explain why the large Amazon catfishes migrate so far upstream to spawn must consider two basic factors. First, what prevents these catfish from using the vast floodplains as nursery habitats, thus avoiding the necessity of using the estuary, at least exclusively? Second, what prevents piramutaba and dourada from spawning in the estuary?

The floodplains of the muddy water rivers are important nursery habitats for many fish species, including the most important migratory characins. The many surveys, including our own, that have been made of Amazon floodplains show that young piramutaba and dourada are absent from these habitats. It thus seems logical to assume that there is something inimical to these fish in floodplain waters. We have no quantitative evidence as to which factor or factors might be involved but offer a review of the possibilities below.

Oxygen

Floodplain waters become very low in dissolved oxygen during certain periods of the year, and the dourada and piramutaba may have no or very little tolerance for anoxic conditions. Fish that depend on the floodplain for nursery and other functions have been shown to have physiological and/or behavioral adaptations to deal with oxygen-poor waters (Junk, Soares, and Carvalho 1983). River channels and the estuary, on the other hand, have excellent oxygen levels because of constant mixing by winds, currents, and/or tides.

Competition

Floodplains are the main nurseries and feeding habitats for the most abundant fish in the Amazon. Competition for food or space resources from characins, cichlids, catfishes, and many other groups of fishes could explain why piramutaba and dourada do not use floodplains as nursery habitats. This hypothesis, however, will be very difficult to test by practical means.

Predation

Bayley (1983, 1988, 1989) has shown that predation is the factor accounting for the most mortality among young fish populations in the Amazon River floodplain near Manaus. It is still unclear whether juvenile piramutaba and dourada suffer high predation in the estuary, although dourada are known to prey to some extent on piramutaba. It is possible that both dourada and piramutaba might suffer less predation in the estuary than would be the case in floodplain waters if they used those habitats. Reid (1986) found that the young of *Sorubim lima*, a medium-size pimelodid catfish of the same group as dourada and piramutaba, have cryptic coloration; *Sorubim lima* also schools and migrates in muddy rivers in the Amazon (Goulding 1981). The young of neither dourada nor piramutaba have cryptic coloration, however, and furthermore they actively pursue their prey. They would thus be highly vulnerable to predation in floodplain waters with their present coloration. It is possible that cryptic coloration is a necessary adaptation for the young of pimelodid catfishes that use the floodplains.

Disease and Parasites
Vernon Thatcher and his colleagues at INPA have shown that floodplain fishes are vulnerable to heavy parasitism (Thatcher 1991). Nearly all floodplain fish species have host-specific macroparasites (e.g., various worm and crustacean groups). It seems unlikely that floodplain macroparasites of other fish species would attack dourada or piramutaba. Less is known about pathogenic bacteria and fungi and almost nothing about viruses that attack Amazonian fishes. Until more is known little can be said about disease differences that might exist between floodplains (quiet waters) and river channels (running water).

As noted above, young dourada are known to prey on young piramutaba, but only after these fish are several weeks old. Reduced predation on eggs and yolk-sac larvae may have led to the evolution of populations that spawn away from the estuary. Ironically, then, both species may migrate upstream in order to place their larvae away from the young of the other species. This, however, raises another question: Why do these fish need to migrate so far? Why don't they just spawn in the central Amazon area, thereby expending less energy for migration and investing more in gonad development?

In the case of dourada, migration out of the estuary may have evolved to prevent intraspecific competition for food between juvenile and adult size classes. Alternatively, there may be more prey in river channels for preadult and adult dourada than is found in the estuary. This would appear not be the case with the piramutaba because all size classes are present in the estuary.

In chapter 6, we showed that dourada and piramutaba feed heavily on midsize fish found in Amazon river channels. None of the prey of inland waters is important in the estuary. Dourada and piramutaba juveniles and piramutaba adults thus experience a complete shift in the types of prey species they eat when they leave the estuary. Piramutaba are thought to return to the estuary at the beginning of the floods. When the entire estuary once again becomes freshwater, there is a greatly expanded environment where piramutaba of all size classes can feed. In great contrast to piramutaba, larger size classes of dourada remain in the central and western Amazon. The dourada is a larger fish and may need larger prey to maintain its growth rate. River channels offer this prey on a seasonal basis.

Fish captured in the central Amazon are at least one to two years younger on average than populations captured in the Rio Caquetá of Colombia. Based on growth calculations, we estimate that dourada begin migrating out of the estuary at a mean age of three years. They spend at least a year feeding in central Amazon rivers and then migrate to headwater regions where they spawn. Dourada measurements reported for the Rio Mamoré, Bolivia, at least 3,100 km upstream of the estuary, however, also show that preadults are found in headwater regions, at least in the Rio Madeira basin (Loubens and Aquim 1986). Preadults are also known in the Rio Caquetá and Amazon River near Leticia (Muñoz Sosa 1993; Salinas 1994). It is possible that preadult dourada (less than about 110 cm) arrive in the western Amazon a year or more before they spawn for the first time.

Amazon fishermen maintain that large dourada do not return downstream. The only place we could test this observation was at the Teotônio rapids of the upper Rio Madeira. All large fish migrating upstream at these rapids are easily noticed by fishermen at any time of the year. If there were downstream migrations of large fish that went unnoticed, they would have to occur during the height of the floods, when dourada might be able to negotiate the cataracts in midstream. To go unnoticed they would also have to descend individually, as schools would surely be seen and exploited. Also, these large individuals would be moving downstream when schools of smaller size classes were migrating upstream. We believe that these downstream movements take place but that they are sporadic and involve only part of the mature population. This explains why large, ripe individuals are occasionally captured in the central Amazon. Large dourada have never been reported or captured in the estuary. We hypothesize that young (one to three years old) and sexually mature adult (more than four years old) populations are, for all practical purposes, geographically separated.

MANAGEMENT: POSSIBLE AND NECESSARY

Scientists have pointed out the difficulty of managing the fisheries based on the large species of the Amazon (e.g., Bayley 1981), in view of the complexity of the fish fauna, the presence of poorly trained regulatory personnel, and the lack of historical statistical data. Goulding (1983) and Barthem (1990a, 1990b) have emphasized that migratory species must be managed if present yields of relatively high-value fish are to be maintained. A large number of people depend on catfish for employment and nutrition, and it is unclear whether these fish can be substituted in the estuary with other species.

Most of the fishing effort (or overexploitation) consists of industrial boats restricted to the estuary. Reducing fishing could thus be very straightforward: merely a matter of reducing the number of industrial boats allowed to exploit the estuary. This would be simple enough to achieve, because, unlike smaller boats (which at present are not a threat), industrial vessels require special docking facilities and so cannot hide from authorities. Because the nurseries of the piramutaba and dourada are confined to the estuary, which means that young fish can only be exploited on a large scale in this relatively restricted region, reducing fishing effort in this area would also protect young populations.

The migratory model for large catfish presented in this book shows that international agreements are needed to protect these species in the long run. The lifelong habitat of dourada and piramutaba, at least, as well as probably several other large but economically less important catfish species as well, spans Brazil, Colombia, Peru, Bolivia, and Ecuador. The nursery habitats of dourada and piramutaba are restricted to the Amazon estuary—Brazilian territory. Overexploitation of these fish in Brazil would thus lead to reduced populations in the other countries.

At the present time, we do not believe that fishing in the upper Amazon, the spawning region, is at dangerous levels. On the other hand, pollution, contamination, or any major form of aquatic environmental degradation in Colombia and Peru especially and in Bolivia, Ecuador, and Brazil to a lesser extent would affect the spawning habitats of these fish. Although the migratory catfish are not important in Ecuador, this country, too, must be included in any overall international agreement. Oil pollution has been a problem in Ecuador, although downstream damage has not reached as far as Brazil. Any major oil spill reaching rivers would undoubtedly affect a large area downstream.

In terms of gear regulations, we believe that only two basic steps need to be taken at this time. First, most of the piramutaba catch in the estuary is taken with otter trawls using 5–10 cm mesh on the cod end of the net. The size of the mesh should be increased to 12 cm to protect small size classes of piramutaba and prevent the needless destruction of other small fish. Second, as the migratory behavior of piramutaba and dourada have become better known in the last decade as a result of increased fishing effort, there is now discussion about using sonar and trawls in the Amazon River channel to locate schools. Brazilian law currently prohibits the use of trawls in river channels, and this restriction must be maintained and reemphasized. This will be especially timely when industrial fishing in the estuary is reduced, which may lead to increased exploitation of the migratory schools when they are in the river channels.

Estuaries on all continents have suffered dramatic ecological changes during this century (Day et al. 1989). There is still time to design programs for the Amazon estuary that would prevent the ecological problems associated with many of the world's rivers. The estuary includes not only the huge open waters on either side of the island of Marajó but also the tidal flooded forests and streams of the archipelagoes and mainland. At present, little is known about the ecology of the Amazon estuary, though heavy logging of tidal forests is one threat that is already apparent. Floodplain forests play an important role throughout the Amazon in providing shelter and food for fish at some stage in their lives (Goulding 1980, 1993; Goulding, Smith, and Mahar 1996). Many fish, crustacean, and other animal species of the estuary depend on flooded habitats, and in this work, we have presented evidence that young dourada and piramutaba use open waters, estuarine streams, and inundated forests as feeding habitats (Barthem 1990b). It is imperative that tidal forests and the streams running through them be protected as part of the nursery habitats of young catfish.

As a group, migratory fishes are the most heavily exploited fisheries in the Amazon, and it is necessary to manage these species over their entire ranges. In the case of dourada and piramutaba, nearly 10,000 km of muddy water rivers may be included in the migratory range of the many schools that move upstream every year and disperse in the many tributaries. We have also shown that the Amazon estuary and inland waters are tightly linked ecologically in the lives of these two large catfishes. What is needed to manage these important fish and fisheries will be a community: of federal officials, scientists, local fishermen's cooperatives, and business interests. This work should provide a foundation on which to build such a community.

Bibliography

Anonymous. 1981. Pesqueiros acabam com a piramutaba. *O Liberal* 26 (4): 81.

Anonymous. 1988. Perfil estatístico das espécies mais vendidas. *Revista CACEX* 23 (1,075).

Araujo-Lima, C. A. R. M. 1990. Larval development and reproductive strategies of Amazonian fishes. Ph.D. diss., University of Stirling, Scotland.

Araujo-Lima, C. A. R. M., B. R. Forsberg, R. Victoria, and L. Martinelli. 1986. Energy sources for detritivorous fishes in the Amazon. *Science* 234:1256–58.

Arboleda, A. L. 1984. Estudio pesquero de los grandes bagres del río Caquetá. Centro de Investigaciónes Científicas, Universidad Jorge Tadeo Lozano, Santa Fé de Bogotá.

Baker, R. R. 1978. *The Evolutionary Ecology of Animal Migration.* New York: Holmes and Meier.

Barbosa, R. P. 1962. Rios brasileiros com mais de 500 km de extensão. *Revista Brasileira de Geografia* 1 (126): 134.

Barletta, M. 1995. Estudo da comunidade de peixes bentônicos em três áreas do canal principal, próximos à confluência dos Rio Negro e Solimões—Amazonas (Amazônia Central—Brasil). Master's thesis, Universidade do Amazonas, Manaus.

Barthem, R. B. 1984. Pesca experimental e seletividade de redes de espera para espécies de peixes amazônicos. *Boletim do Museu Paraense Emilio Goeldi (Zoologia)* 1 (1): 57–88.

Barthem, R. B. 1985. Ocorrência, distribuição e biologia dos peixes da baia de Marajó, estuário amazônico. *Boletim do Museu Paraense Emilio Goeldi (Zoologia)* 2 (1): 49–69.

Barthem, R. B. 1987. Uso de redes de espera no estudo de rítmos circadianos de algumas espécies de peixes nos lagos de várzea do Rio Solimões. *Revista Brasileira de Zoologia, São Paulo* 31 (5): 409–22.

Barthem, R. B. 1990a. Descrição da pesca da piramutaba (*Brachyplatystoma vaillantii,* Pimelodidae) no estuário e na calha do Rio Amazonas. *Boletim do Museu Paraense Emilio Goeldi (Antropologia)* 6 (1): 117–30.

Barthem, R. B. 1990b. Ecologia e pesca da piramutaba (*Brachyplatystoma vaillantii*). Ph.D. diss., Universidade de São Paulo, Rio Claro.

Barthem, R. B., M. Ribeiro, and M. Petrere Jr. 1991. Life strategies of some long-distance migratory catfish in relation of hydroelectric dams in the Amazon basin. *Biological Conservation* 55:339–45.

Barthem, R. B., H. Guerra, and M. Valderrama. 1995. *Diagnóstico de los recursos hidrobiológicos de la Amazonía.* 2d ed. Iquitos, Peru: Secretaria Pro Tempore.

Barthem, R. B. and H. O. Schwassmann. 1994. The Amazon river influence over the seasonal displacement of the salty wedges in the Tocantins estuary, Brazil, 1983–1985. *Boletim do Museu Paraense Emilio Goeldi (Zoologia)* 10 (1): 119–30.

Bayley, P. B. 1970. *The Ecology and Fisheries of the River Pilcomayo in Bolivia.* Santa Cruz, Bolivia: Ministerio de Asuntos Campesinos y Agricultura.

Bayley, P. B. 1973. Studies on the migratory characin, *Prochilodus platensis* Holmberg, 1889 (Pisces, Characoidei) in the river Pilcomayo, South America. *Journal of Fish Biology* 5:25–40.

Bayley, P. B. 1981. Fish yield from the Amazon in Brazil: Comparison with African river yields and management possibilities. *Transactions of the American Fisheries Society* 110:351–59.

Bayley, P. B. 1983. Central Amazon fish populations: Biomass, production and some dynamic characteristics. Ph.D. diss., Dalhousie University.

Bayley, P. B. 1988. Factors affecting growth rates of young floodplain fishes: Seasonality and Density-Dependence. *Environmental Biology of Fishes* 21:127–42.

Bayley, P. B. 1989. Aquatic environments in the Amazon basin, with an analysis of carbon sources, fish production, and yield. *Canadian Special Publications in Fisheries and Aquatic Science* 106:399–408.

Bayley, P. B. and M. Petrere Jr. 1989. Amazon fisheries: Assessment methods, current status and management options. *Canadian Special Publications in Fisheries and Aquatic Science* 106:385–98.

Begossi, A. and F. M. S. Braga. 1992. Food taboos and folk medicine among fishermen from the Tocantins river (Brazil). *Amazoniana* 12 (1): 101–18.

Begossi, A. and J. C. Garavello. 1990. Notes on the ethnoichthyology from Tocantins river (Brazil). *Acta Amazonica* 20 (1): 341–52.

Boischio, A. M. P. 1992. Produção pesqueira em Porto Velho, Rondônia (1984–89): Alguns aspectos ecológicos das espécies comercialmente relevantes. *Acta Amazonica* 22 (1): 163–72.

Boischio, A. M. P. 1995. Mercury exposure through fish consumption by the upper Madeira River population, Brazil 1991. *Ecosystem Health* 1 (3): 177–92.

Bonetto, A. A. and C. Pignalberi. 1964. Nuevos aportes al conocimiento de las migraciónes de los peces en los rios mesopotamicos de la Republica Argentina. *Communicaciónes Instituto Nacional Limnologia* 1:1–14.

Bonetto, A. A., C. Pignalberi, and E. C. Yuan. 1971. Informaciónes complentarias sobre migraciónes de peces en la cuenca del Plata. *Physis* 30 (81): 505–20.

Borges, G. A. 1986. Ecologia de três espécies do gênero *Brycon* Muller & Trochel, 1844 (Pisces, Characiformes) no Rio Negro–Amazonas, com ênfase na caracterização taxonômica e alimentação. Master's thesis, INPA/FUA, Manaus.

Boulenger, G. A. 1898. On a collection of fishes from the rio Juruá, Brazil. *Transactions of the Zoological Society, London* 14:421–28.

Britski, H. A. 1981. Sobre um novo gênero e espécie de Sorubiminae da Amazônia (Pisces, Siluriformes). *Papeis Avulos de Zoologia, São Paulo* 34 (7): 109–14.

Britto, R. C. C., D. A. B. Santos, M. A. S. F. Torres, and M. S. Braga. 1975. *A pesca empresarial do Pará*. Belém: IDESP.

Burr, B. M. and R. L. Mayden. 1982. Life history of the brindled madtom *Nocturus miurus* in Mill Creek, Illinois (Pisces: Ictaluridae). *American Midland Naturalist* 107 (1): 25–41.

CACEX–Banco do Brasil. 1980. Principais produtos exportados pelo estado do Pará. *Secretaria de Estado da Fazenda/Coordenadoria de Informações Econômicos Fiscais*: 1–25.

Carvalho, J. L and B. Merona. 1986. Estudos sobre dois peixes migratórios do baixo Tocantins, antes do fechamento da barragem de Tucuruí. *Amazoniana* 9 (4): 595–607.

Castillo, O. R. G. 1978. Pesca: Artes e métodos de captura industrial no estado do Pará, Brasil. *Boletim da Faculdade das Ciências do Pará, Belém* 10:93–112.

Castro, D. M. 1984. Hallazgo del bagre *Merodontotus tigrinus* en la Amazonia colombiana. *Boletin de La Faculdad de Biologia Mariña* 3:21–24.

Castro, D. M. 1986. Los bagres de la subfamilia Sorubiminae de la Orinoquia y Amazonia colombiana (Siluriformes—Pimelodidae). *Boletim Ecotropica* 13:1–39.

Compagno, L. J. V. 1984. An annotated and illustrated catalogue of shark species known to date. *Fao Fisheries Synopsis—Part 2* 4 (125): 477–82.

COPRAPHI. 1984. *Hidrologia e Climatologia na Região Amazônica Brasileira: Informação Disponível e Atividades em Desenvolvimento*. Manaus: COPRAPHI.

Curtin, T. B. and R. V. Legeckis. 1986. Physical observations in the plume region of the Amazon river during peak discharge: I. Surface variability. *Continental Shelf Research* 6 (1/2): 31–51.

Cushing, D. H. and F. R. Harden-Jones. 1968. Why do fish school? *Nature* 218:918–20.

Day, J. A. and B. R. Davies. 1986. The Amazon River system. In B. R. Davies and K. F. Walker, eds., *The Ecology of River Systems*, 289–317. Dordrecht: Dr. W. Junk Publishers.

Day, J. W., C. A. S. Hall, W. M. Kemp, and A. Yáñez-Arancibia. 1989. *Estuarine Ecology*. New York: Wiley.

Dias-Neto, J. and J. Mesquita. 1988. Potencialidade e explotação dos recursos pesqueiros do Brasil. *Ciência e Cultura* 40 (5): 427–41.

Dias-Neto, J., F. G. Damasceno, and A. C. de P. Pontes. 1985. Biologia e pesca da piramutaba, *Brachyplatystoma vaillantii*, Valenciennes, na Região Norte do Brasil. *SUDEPE Série Documentos Técnicos* 35:47–112.

Diegues, F. M. F. 1972. Introdução à oceanografia do estuário amazônico. *Anais do XXVI Congresso Brasileiro de Geologia*, 2:301–17. Belém: Sociedade Brasileira de Geologia.

Egler, W. A. and H. O. Schwassmann. 1962. Limnological studies in the Amazon estuary. *Boletim do Museu Paraense Emilio Goeldi (Nova Série Avulsa)* 1:2–25.

Eigenmann, C. H. and R. S. Eigenmann. 1890. A revision of South American Nematognathi, or catfishes. *Occasional Papers of the California Academy of Sciences* 1:1–508.

Eigenmann, C. H. and R. S. Eigenmann. 1971. *South American Nematognathi, or Cat-Fishes*. 1890. Reprint. New York: Johnson Reprint Corporation.

Eisma, D. and H. W. Marel. 1971. Marine muds along the Guyana coast and their origin from the Amazon basin. *Contributions to Mineralogy and Petrology* 31:321–34.

Forsberg, B., C. A. R. M. Araujo-Lima, L. A. Martinelli, R. L. Victoria, and J. A. Bonassi. 1993. Autotrophic carbon sources for fish of the central Amazon. *Ecology* 74:643–52.

Furtado, L. G. 1981. Pesca artesanal: Um delineamento de sua história no Pará. *Boletim do Museu Paraense Emilio Goeldi (Antropologia)* 79:1–50.

Furtado, L. G. 1987. *Curralistas e Redeiros de Marudá, Pescadores do Litoral do Pará.* Belém: Ministério da Ciência e Tecnologia.

Garrick, J. A. F. 1982. *Sharks of the genus Carcharhinus.* NMFS Circular 445. Washington, D.C.: U.S. Department of Commerce.

Gibbs, R. J. 1967. The geochemistry of the Amazon river system. Part I: The factors that control the salinity and the composition and concentration of the suspended solids. *Bulletin of the Geological Society of America* 78 (10): 1203–32.

Godoy, M. P. 1959. Age, growth, sexual maturity, behaviour, migration, tagging and transplantation of the curimbatá (*Prochilodus scrofa* Steindachner, 1881) of the Mogi Guassu river, S. Paulo state, Brasil. *Anais de Academia Brasileira de Ciências* 31:447–77.

Godoy, M. P. 1967. Dez anos de observações sobre periodicidade migratória de peixes do Rio Mogi Guassu. *Revista Brasileira de Biologia* 27:1–12.

Godoy, M. P. 1975. *Peixes do Brasil, Subordem Characoidei: Bacia do Rio Mogi Guassu.* Rio de Janeiro: CNPq.

Godoy, M. P. 1979. Marcarção e migração da piramutaba *Brachyplatystoma vaillantii* (Val., 1840) na bacia amazônica (Pará e Amazonas), Brasil (Pisces, Nematognathi, Pimelodidae). *Boletim da Faculdade de Ciências do Pará, Belém* 11:1–21.

Goeldi, E. A. 1897. A piraíba, gigantesco siluroideo do Amazonas. *Boletim do Museu Paraense* 3:181–94.

Goulding, M. 1979. *Ecologia da Pesca do Rio Madeira.* Manaus: CNPq/INPA.

Goulding, M. 1980. *The Fishes and the Forest: Explorations in Amazonian Natural History.* Berkeley: University of California Press.

Goulding, M. 1981. *Man and Fisheries on an Amazon Frontier.* The Hague: Dr. W. Junk Publishers.

Goulding, M. 1983. Amazonian fisheries. In E. F. Moran, ed., *The Dilemma of Amazonian Development*, 189–210. Boulder, Colo.: Westview.

Goulding, M. 1988. Ecology and management of migratory food fishes of the Amazon Basin. In F. Almeda and C. M. Pringle, eds., *Tropical Rainforests: Diversity and Conservation*, 71–85. San Francisco: California Academy of Sciences.

Goulding, M. 1989. *Amazon: The Flooded Forest.* London: The BBC.

Goulding, M. 1993. Flooded forests of the Amazon. *Scientific American* 266 (3): 114–20.

Goulding, M., and M. L. Carvalho. 1982. Life history and management of the tambaqui (*Colossoma macropomum*, Characidae): An important Amazonian food fish. *Revista Brasileira de Zoologia* 1 (2): 107–33.

Goulding, M., M. L. Carvalho, and E. G. Ferreira. 1988. *Rio Negro: Rich Life in Poor Water: Amazonian Diversity and Foodchain Ecology As Seen Through Fish Communities.* The Hague: SPB Academic Publishing.

Goulding, M., N. J. H. Smith, and D. Mahar. 1996. *Floods of Fortune: Ecology and Economy Along the Amazon.* New York: Columbia University Press.

Harden-Jones, F. R. 1985. A view from the ocean. In F. R. Harden-Jones, ed., *Mechanisms of Migration in Fishes*, 1–26. New York: Plenum.

Hoorn, C., J. Guerrero, and G. A. Sarmiento. 1995. Andean tectonics as a cause for changing drainage patterns in Miocene northern South America. *Geology* 23 (3): 237–40.

Ibarra, M. and D. J. Stewart. 1989. Longitudinal zonation of sandy beach fishes in the Napo river basin, eastern Ecuador. *Copeia*, no. 2: 364–81.

Ihering, R. 1928. *Da Vida dos Peixes*. São Paulo: Companhia Melhoramentos de São Paulo.

Junk, W. J. 1970. Investigations on the ecology and production-biology of the "floating meadows" (Paspalo-Echinochloetum) on the middle Amazon. Part I: The floating vegetation and its ecology. *Amazoniana* 2:449–95.

Junk, W. J. 1973. Investigations on the ecology and production-biology of the "floating meadows" (Paspalo-Echinocloetum) on the middle Amazon. Part II: The aquatic fauna in the root zone of floating vegetation. *Amazoniana* 4:9–102.

Junk, W. J., G. M. Soares, and F. M. Carvalho. 1983. Distribution of fish species in a lake of the Amazon river floodplain near Manaus (Lago Camaleão) with special reference to extreme oxygen conditions. *Amazoniana* 7:397–431.

Krebs, C. J. 1989. *Ecological Methodology*. New York: Harper and Row.

Leggett, W. C. 1977. The ecology of fish migrations. *Annual Review of Ecology and Systematics* 8:285–308.

Leggett, W. C. 1985. Fish migrations in coastal and estuarine environments: A call for new approaches to the study of an old problem. In W. C. Leggett, ed., *Mechanisms of Migration in Fishes*, 159–78. New York: Plenum.

Loubens, G. and J. L. Aquim. 1986. Sexualidad y reproducción de los principales peces de la cuenca del Rio Mamoré, Beni, Bolivia. *Informe Científico (ORSTOM, CORDEBENI, UTB, Trinidad, Bolivia)* 5: 1–20.

Loureiro, V. R. 1985. *Os Parceiros do Mar. Natureza e Conflito Social na Pesca Em Amazônia*. Belém: CNPq/Museu Paraense Emilio Goeldi.

Lowe-McConnell, R. H. 1964. The fishes of the Rupununi savanna district of British Guiana. Pt. 1: Groupings of fish species and effects of the seasonal cycles on the fish. *Journal of the Linnean Society (Zoology)* 45:103–44.

Lowe-McConnell, R. H. 1967. Some factors affecting fish populations in Amazonian waters. *Atas do Simpósio Sobre a Biota Amazônica (Zoologia)* 7:177–86.

Lowe-McConnell, R. H. 1975. *Fish Communities in Tropical Freshwaters: Their Distribution, Ecology and Evolution*. London: Longman.

Lowe-McConnell, R. H. 1977. *Ecology of Fishes in Tropical Waters*. London: Edward Arnold.

Lowe-McConnell, R. H. 1979. Ecological aspects of seasonality in fishes of tropical waters. *Symposia of the Zoological Society of London* 44:219–41.

Lowe-McConnell, R. H. 1984. The status of studies on South American freshwater food fishes. In T. Zaret, ed., *Evolutionary Ecology of Neotropical Freshwater Fishes*, 139–56. The Hague: Dr. W. Junk Publishers.

Lowe-McConnell, R. H. 1987. *Ecological Studies in Tropical Fish Communities*. Cambridge: Cambridge University Press.

Lundberg, J. G., W. M. Lewis Jr., J. F. Saunders, and F. Magio-Leccia. 1987. A major food web component in the Orinoco river channel: Evidence from planktivorous electric fishes. *Science* 237:81–83.

Lundberg, J. G., A. Machado-Allison, and R. F. Kay. 1986. Miocene characid fishes from Colombia: Evolutionary stasis and extirpation. *Science* 234:208–9.

McCleave, J. D., ed. 1985. *Mechanisms of Migration in Fishes*. New York: Plenum.

McDowall, R. M. 1988. *Diadromy in Fishes*. London: Croom Hill.

Machado-Allison, A. 1987. *Los Peces de Los Llanos de Venezuela*. Caracas: Universidad Central de Venezuela.

Mago-Leccia, F. 1970. *Lista de Los Peces de Venezuela, Incluyendo un Estudio Preliminar Sobre La Ictiogeogragrafia del Pais*. Caracas: Ministerio de Agricultura e Cria.

Meade, R., J. M. Rayol, S. C. Conceição, and J. R. G. Natividade. 1991. Backwater effects in the Amazon River basin of Brazil. *Environmental Geology and Water Science* 18 (2): 105–14.

Mees, G. F. 1974. *The Auchenipteridae and Pimelodidae of Suriname (Pisces, Nematognathi)*. Leiden: E. J. Brill.

Menezes, N. A. 1970. Distribuição e origem da fauna de peixes de água doce das grandes bacias fluviais do Brasil. In Commisão Interestadual Bacia Paraná-Uruguai, ed., *Poluição e Piscicultura*, 73–78. São Paulo: Publicações Commisão Interestadual Bacia Paraná–Uruguai.

Menezes, N. A. and A. E. Vazzoler. 1992. Reproductive characteristics of Characiformes. In W. C. Hamlett, ed., *Reproductive Biology of South American Vertebrates*, 101–14. New York: Springer.

Miller, J. M, J. P. Reed, and L. J. Pietrafesa. 1985. Patterns, mechanisms and approaches to the study of migrations of estuarine-dependent fish larvae and juveniles. In J. D. McCleave, G. P. Arnold, J. J. Dodson, and W. H. Neil, eds., *Mechanisms of Migration in Fishes*, 209–26. New York: Plenum.

Milliman, J. D. and R. H. Meade. 1983. World-wide delivery of river sediment to the oceans. *Journal of Geology* 91 (1): 1–21.

Muñoz Sosa, D. L. 1993. Evaluación de la actividad pesquera en el bajo Caquetá, entre Araracuara y La Pedrera, Amazonas–Colombia. *Fundación Puerto Rastrojo: Informe Técnico*: 1–128.

Myers, G. S. 1941. A new name for *Taenionema*, a genus of American siluroid fishes. *Stanford Ichthyological Bulletin* 2:88.

Myers, G. S. 1949. Usage of anadromous, catadromous and allied terms for migratory fishes. *Copeia*, no. 2: 89–96.

Myers, G. S. 1952. Sharks and sawfishes in the Amazon. *Copeia*, no. 4: 268–69.

Neto, J. D., J. E. V. Evangelista, and F. A. P. Freitas. 1981. Experimento de seletividade com rede de arrasto para piramutaba, *Brachyplatystoma vaillantii*, Valenciennes. *Série Documentos Técnicos* 35: 3–46.

Nikolsky, G. V. 1963. *The Ecology of Fishes*. London: Academic Press.

Northcote, T. G. 1985. Mechanisms of fish migrations in rivers. In J. D. McCleave, ed., *Mechanisms of Migration in Fishes*, 317–56. New York: Plenum.

Novoa, D. 1982. *Los Recursos Pesqueros del Rio Orinoco y Su Explotación*. Caracas: Corporación Venezolana de Guayana.

Novoa, D. F. 1989. The multispecies fisheries of the Orinoco river: Development, present status, and management strategies. *Proceedings of the International Large River Symposium* 106:345–56.

Partridge, B. L. 1982. The structure and function of fish schools. *Scientific American* 246 (6): 90–126.

Penner, M. E. S. 1980. A pesca no nordeste amazônico. *Raizes* 1 (1): 47–56.

Petrere Jr., M. 1978a. Pesca e esforço de pesca no estado do Amazonas. I. Esforço e captura por unidade de esforço. *Acta Amazonica* 8 (3): 439–54.

Petrere Jr., M. 1978b. Pesca e esforço de pesca no estado do Amazonas. II. Locais, aparelhos de captura e estatística de desembarque. *Acta Amazonica* 8 (3): 1–54.

Petrere Jr., M. 1985a. A pesca comercial no Rio Solimões–Amazonas e seus afluentes: Análise dos informos do pescado desembarcado no mercado municipal de Manaus (1976–78). *Ciência e Cultura* 37:1987–99.

Petrere Jr., M. 1985b. Migraciónes de peces de água dulce en America Latina: Algunos comentários. *Copescal Documento Ocasional* 1:1–31.

Reid, S. 1983. La biologia de los bagres rayados *Pseudoplatystoma fasciatum* y *P. tigrinum* en la cuenca del rio Apure, Venezuela. *Revista Unellez de Ciencia y Tecnologia* 1 (1): 13–41.

Reid, S. B. 1986. Cryptic adaptations of small juvenile catfishes *Sorubim lima* (Pimelodidae) in Venezuela. *Biotropica* 18 (1): 86–88.

Ribeiro, M. C. L. B. 1983. As migrações de jaraquis (Pisces, Prochilodontidae) no Rio Negro, Amazonas, Brasil. Master's thesis. INPA/FUA, Manaus.

Ribeiro, M. C. L. B. 1984. Composição por comprimento e idade de cardumes de *Semaprochilodus* no baixo Rio Negro, Amazonas. *Resumos. XI Congresso Brasileiro de Zoologia, Belém* (February 12–17): 204–5.

Ribeiro, M. C. L. B. and M. Petrere Jr. 1990. Fisheries ecology and management of the jaraqui (*Semaprochilodus taeniurus, S. insignis*) in central Amazônia. *Regulated Rivers: Research and Management* 5:195–215.

Ribeiro, M. C. L. B., M. Petrere Jr., and A. A. Juras. 1995. Ecological integrity and fisheries ecology of the Araguaia-Tocantins river basin, Brazil. *Regulated Rivers: Research and Management* 10:31–45.

Richey, J. E., L. A. Mertes, and R. L. Victoria. 1989. Sources and routing of the Amazon river floodwave. *Global Biogeochemical Cycles* 3:191–204.

Roberts, T. 1972. Ecology of fishes in the Amazon and Congo basins. *Bulletin of the Museum of Comparative Zoology, Harvard* 143:117–47.

Roberts, T. R. 1973. Ecology of fishes in the Amazon and Congo basins. In B. J. Meggers, E. S. Ayensu, and W. D. Duckworth, eds., *Tropical Forest Ecosystems in Africa and South America: A Comparative Review*, 239–54. Washington, D.C.: Smithsonian Institution Press.

Rodriguez Fernandez, R. 1991. *Bagres, Malleros e Cuerderos en El Bajo Rio Caquetá*. Bogotá: Tropenbos.

Rosa, R. S. 1985. A systematic revision of the South American freshwater stingrays (Chondrichthyes: Potamotrygonidae). Ph.D. diss., College of William and Mary, Virginia.

Ryther, J. H., D. W. Menzel, and N. Cordin. 1967. Influence of the Amazon river outflow on the ecology of the western tropical Atlantic: I. Hydrography and nutrient chemistry. *Journal of Marine Research* 25 (1): 69–83.

Salati, E., W. J. Junk, H. O. Schubart, and A. E. Oliveira. 1983. *Amazônia: Desenvolvimento, Integração e Ecologia*. São Paulo: Brasiliense/CNPq.

Salati, E. and P. B. Vose. 1984. Amazon basin: A system in equilibrium. *Science* 235:1062–64.

Salinas, Y. C. 1994. Aspectos de la biologia pesquera de las poblaciónes de los grandes bagres (Ostariophysi: Siluriformes, Pimelodidae) en el sector colombiano del rio Amazonas. Graduate thesis, Universidad Pedagogica Nacional, Santafé de Bogotá.

Santos, G. M. 1986. Composição do pescado e situação da pesca no estado de Rondônia. *Acta Amazonia* 16 (17): 43–84.

Silva, V. M. F. 1983. Ecologia alimentar dos golfinhos da Amazônia. Master's thesis, INPA, Manaus.

Sioli, H. 1966. General features of the delta of the Amazon. *Humid Tropics Research. Proceedings, Dacca Symposium*:381–90.

Smith, N. J. H. 1979. *A Pesca no Rio Amazonas*. Manaus: Instituto Nacional de Pesquisas da Amazônia.

Smith, N. J. H. 1981. *Man, Fishes and the Amazon*. New York: Columbia University Press.

Smith, R. J. F. 1985. *The Control of Fish Migration*. Berlin: Springer.

Steindachner, F. 1909. Über *Brachyplatystoma* (*Taenionema*) *platynema* Blgr. aus der Umgebung von Para. *Anzeiger der Kaiserlichen Akademie Wissenschaft (Wien)* 26:9–10.

Superintendência do Desenvolvimento da Pesca (SUDEPE). 1979. Relatório preliminar da reunião do grupo permanente de estudo sobre a piramutaba, 28 a 30 de março. Manuscript.

Superintendência do Desenvolvimento da Pesca (SUDEPE). 1980. Relatório técnico anual. Manuscript.

Superintendência do Desenvolvimento da Pesca (SUDEPE). 1985. *Relatório do subgrupo de biologia pesqueira e technologia da pesca da reunião do grupo permanente de estudos sobre piramutaba* (March):1–20.

Taphorn, D. C. 1992. The characiform fishes of the Apure river drainage, Venezuela. *Biollania* (special volume) 4:1–537.

Thatcher, V. 1991. Amazon fish parasites. *Amazoniana* 3/4:263–555.

Thorson, T. B. 1972. The status of the bull shark, *Carcharhinus leucas*, in the Amazon river. *Copeia*, no. 3: 601–5.

Thorson, T. B. 1973. Body fluid solutes of juveniles and adults of the euryhaline bull shark *Carcharhinus leucas* from freshwater and saline environments. *Physiological Zoology* 46 (1): 29–42.

Thorson, T. B. 1974. Occurrence of the sawfish, *Pristis perotteti*, in the Amazon river, with notes on *P. pectinatus*. *Copeia*, no. 2: 560–64.

Vari, R. P. 1995. The neotropical fish family Ctenoluciidae (Teleostei: Ostariophysi: Characiformes): Supra and intrafamilial phylogenetic relationships, with a revisionary study. *Smithsonian Contributions to Zoology* 564:1–97.

Vazzoler, A. E. A. M. and S. A. Amadio. 1990. Aspectos biológicos de peixes amazônicos. XIII. Estrutura e comportamento de cardumes multiespecíficos de *Semaprochilodus* (Characiformes, Prochilodontidae) no baixo Rio Negro, Amazonas, Brasil. *Revista Brasileira de Biologia* 50 (3): 537–46.

Vazzoler, A. E. A. M., S. A. Amadio, and M. C. Caraciolo-Malta. 1989a. Aspectos biológicos de peixes amazônicos. XI. Reprodução das espécies do gênero *Semaprochilodus* (Characiformes, Prochildontidae) no baixo Rio Negro, Amazonas, Brazil. *Revista Brasileira de Biologia* 49 (1): 165–173.

Vazzoler, A. E. A. M., S. A. Amadio, and M. C. Caraciolo-Malta. 1989b. Aspectos biológicos de peixes amazônicos. XII. Indicadores quantitativos do período de desova das espécies do gênero *Semaprochilodus* (Characiformes, Prochilodontidae) do baixo Rio Negro, Amazonas. *Revista Brasileira de Biologia* 49 (1): 175–81.

Vazzoler, A. E. A. M. and N. A. Menezes. 1992. Síntese de conhecimentos sobre o comportamento reprodutivo dos Characiformes da América do Sul (Teleostei, Ostariophysi). *Revista Brasileira de Biologia* 52 (4): 627–40.

Veríssimo, J. 1895. *A Pesca na Amazônia*. Rio de Janeiro: Livraria Classica Francisco Alves.

Vizotto, L. D. and V. A. Taddei. 1978. Tubarão da Amazônia. *Anais da Academia Brasileira de Ciências (Rio de Janeiro)* 50 (3): 85.

Webb, S. D. 1995. Biological implications of the middle Miocene Amazon seaway. *Science* 269:361–62.

Weitzman, S. H. and R. P. Vari. 1988. Miniaturization in South American freshwater fishes: An overview and discussion. *Proceedings of the Biological Society, Washington* 101 (2): 444–65.

Weitzman, S. H. and M. Weitzman. 1982. Biogeography and evolutionary diversification in Neotropical freshwater fishes, with comments on the refuge theory. In G. T. Prance, ed., *Biological Diversification in the Tropics*, 403–22. New York: Columbia University Press.

Werder, U. and C. E. Alhanati. 1981. Informe sobre um tubarão (*Carcharhinus leucas*) cap-
turado no Amazonas com alguns detalhes de sua morfologia externa. *Acta Amazonica* 11
(1): 193–96.

Zuanon, J. A. S. 1990. Aspectos da biologia, ecologia e pesca de grandes bagres (Pisces:
Siluriformes, Siluroidei) na área da Ilha de Marchantaria–Rio Solimões. U.S. master's
thesis, Instituto Nacional de Pesquisas da Amazônia, Manaus.

Index

Page numbers in italics refer to illustrations, tables, and charts.